A Gallery of Harlem Portraits

Works by Melvin B. Tolson

A Gallery of Harlem Portraits
(completed in 1935, published in 1979)

Rendezvous with America (1944)

Libretto for the Republic of Liberia (1953)

Harlem Gallery: Book I, The Curator (1965)

Melvin B. Tolson

A Gallery
of Harlem Portraits

Edited, with an afterword, by Robert M. Farnsworth

University of Missouri Press
Columbia & London, 1979

Copyright © 1979 by The Curators of the University of Missouri
University of Missouri Press, Columbia, Missouri 65211
Library of Congress Catalog Card Number 79-3939
Printed and bound in the United States of America
All rights reserved

Library of Congress Cataloging in Publication Data

Tolson, Melvin Beaunorus.
    A gallery of Harlem portraits.

    1. Afro-Americans—New York (City)
—Harlem—Poetry.   2.   Harlem, New York (City)
—Description—Poetry.   I.   Farnsworth,
Robert M.   II.   Title.
PS3539.0334G3   811'.5'2   79-3939
ISBN 0-8262-0276-4
ISBN 0-8262-0280-2 pbk.

This book is being published with the assistance of an
award from the American Council of Learned Societies.

Photographs on pp. 239–43, 245–51, and 254 reproduced
courtesy of the Schomburg Center of Research in
Black Culture, The New York Public Library, Astor,
Lenox and Tilden Foundations.

Photographs on pp. 244 and 252–53 reproduced
courtesy of the Van Der Zee Collection,
The Studio Museum in Harlem.

To Ruth Marie Tolson

Contents

Chiaroscuro

Harlem

Diamond Canady
Was stabbed in bed by Little Eva Winn.
Deacon Phineas Bloom
Confessed his adultery on his deathbed.

Dusky Bards,
Heirs of eons of Comedy and Tragedy,
Pass along the streets and alleys of Harlem
Singing ballads of the Dark World:

> When a man has lost his taste fer you,
>   Jest leave dat man alone.
> Says I . . . a dawg won't eat a bone
>   If he don't want de bone.

> I likes de Eyetalian . . . I likes de Jew . . .
> I likes de Chinaman, but I don't like you.

> Happy days are here again.
> Dat's sho' one great big lie.
> Ain't had a beefsteak in so long
> My belly wants to cry.

> Preacher called to bless my home
> An' keep it free from strife.
> Preacher called to bless my home
> An' keep it free from strife.
> Now I's got a peaceful home
> An' de preacher's got my wife.

White cops sho' will beat you up, littlest thing you do.
Black cops make Black Boy feel proud, but dey'll beat you too!

> Rather be a hobo, Lawd,
> Wid a stinkin' breath
> Dan live in de Big House
> Workin' folks to death.

> My two-timin' Mama says to me:
> Daddy, did I let you down?
> Gonna break dat woman's goddamn neck
> Befo' I leaves dis town.

> Black Boy, sing an' clown an' dance,
>   Strutt yo' low-down nigger stuff.
> White Folks sho' will tip you big
>   If you flatters 'em enough.

3

Frederick Judson
Made cigars that pleased General Ulysses Grant.
Soldier Boy
Was decorated by Pancho Villa.
Poker Face Duncan
Killed his rival with a billiard ball.

Vergil Ragsdale,
Dishwasher poet at Mr. Maranto's café,
Who wrote the epic *An African Tragedy*
Burned as trash by Big Sadie's husband . . .
Vergil Ragsdale, the consumptive,
Gulped down a glass of molten gin,
Leaned tipsily against the bar in Duke Huggins's Subway,
Scanned with fever-bright eyes
The horizon of uncouth black faces,
And declaimed in funereal cadences:

"Harlem, O Harlem,
I shall not see the quiet Dawn
When the yellow and brown and black proletarians
Swarm out of stinking dives and fire-trap tenements,
Pour through canyon-streets,
Climb Strivers' Row and Sugar Hill,
Erase the liveried flunkies,
And belly laugh in the rich apartments of the Big Niggers.

"I shall not see the unwashed mob
Hoofing the Lindy Hop in Madame Alpha Devine's drawing room,
Guzzling champagne in Banker Calverton's library,
Bouncing their unperfumed butts upon Miss Briffault's silken beds,
Gorging the roast chicken and eclairs in Editor Speare's kitchen.

"Harlem, O Harlem,
City of the Big Niggers,
Graveyard of the Dark Masses,
Soapbox of the Red Apocalypse . . .
I shall be forgotten like you
Beneath the Debris of Oblivion."

Radicals, prizefighters, actors and deacons,
Beggars, politicians, professors and redcaps,
Bulldikers, Babbitts, racketeers and jig-chasers,
Harlots, crapshooter, workers and pink-chasers,
Artists, dicties, Pullman porters and messiahs . . .
The Curator has hung the likenesses of all
In *A Gallery of Harlem Portraits*.

Gloomy Dean

Sure got the blues this mornin',
An' that rent party last night didn't do me no good.
Tried to drown ma troubles in gin,
But ma troubles keep on climbin'
Like the angels on Jacob's ladder.
Went to bed 'bout four A.M.
An' couldn't sleep none a-tall.

Got up an' walked in Lenox Avenue . . .
Saw the sun risin' an' says to maself:
"Lawdy, Lawdy, when is good luck gonna shine on me?"

Told ma buddies out in the Panhandle . . . West Texas . . .
Never gonna let no woman put a ball-an'-chain on me.
Met a gal from Palm Beach an' ma love come down.
Got drunk two days an' woke up
With that Palm Beach woman in ma bed
An' a marriage license in ma pocket.
Then I worked like hell for that high yellah mama . . .
Givin' her ma check like a damn fool. . . . An' . . .
By Gawd, she runs off with a good-for-nothin' nigger!

Lawdy, Lawdy, women can sure be mean,
Lawdy, Lawdy, two-timin' gals is mean,
Palm Beach woman worst that I has seen!

Some folks say you reap just what you sow,
Preachers say you reap just what you sow,
Gonna get ma gun an' lay that woman low.

5

Miss Eulaline Briffault

High-Hattin' Mama, go an' salt this down:
Never lived the queen who couldn't lose her crown.

Miss Briffault walked briskly up the sordid street,
Lifting her white voile skirt,
With competent fingers,
And drawing it aside
As she passed a chattering group of sweating Negroes.

A wizened Jew with sharp beady eyes
Started to speak to her from the vague doorway
Of a cluttered pawnshop.
But Miss Briffault closed his bearded mouth
With a classical stare.

A dingy black woman, big with child,
Waddled behind a rattletrap baby carriage . . .
Miss Briffault's octoroon lips congealed into a severe line
Curled at the ends like a comma.

Miss Briffault was thinking:
When I was a little girl,
This was a respectable street.
Of course,
That was before the ignorant blacks from the South
And the dirty Jews from the Ghetto
Took possession of Harlem.
Wherever you find an ignorant Negro,
You find a dirty Jew . . .
The carrion and the buzzard!

Diamond Canady

I plays any game
Dat you kin name,
For any amount
Dat you kin count.

He came from Nome, Alaska,
With a diamond in his necktie
Like the headlight on The Broadway Limited,
And a diamond in his ring
Like an evening star;
And when he grinned his all-embracing grin
A diamond illuminated the cavern of his mouth.

He was a gambling man
Who could do more tricks with a deck of cards
Than a monkey with a coconut.

And free-loving women from Nome to Harlem
Swore over their cocktails
That his ways of making love
Surpassed his card tricks.

When Diamond Canady swaggered into a dive,
The sharps became novices
In the presence of a master.
When Diamond Canady favored a woman,
She felt like a commoner honored by a king.

"Love 'em and leave 'em,"
Said Diamond Canady . . .
But when he got ready to cast Little Eva Winn aside
She left him in bed one morning
With a thin knife sticking in his heart.

African China

East is East an' West is West,
You heahs de People say.
But when you mixes East an' South
De devil is to pay.

Mabel worked in the hand laundry of Lou Sing . . .
And her friends laughed derisively
When she married the little yellow man
Whose parables glittered with epigrams.

Along Eighth Avenue
Wise old women said
The marriage would turn out badly
Because it was the marriage of Africa and China. . . .

But that was long, long ago.
Lou Sing says
His Mabel is a dusky passion flower
That has not lost its charm
With the passing of envious years.

And Mabel says
Her Lou Sing is a restful oasis . . .
Blessed by Allah . . .
In the desert of Harlem manhood.

Lou Sing and Mabel are proud of their love child,
A son with the Oriental features of the father
And the ebony skin of the mother . . .
And the children along Eighth Avenue call the son
African China.

Nig Grinde

He was a skinny black Arab
Whose mother worked ten hours a day
In a badly ventilated and poorly lighted
Paper-box-making plant.
She was a wretched consumptive,
And the unsanitary toilets sickened her.

Brought before a juvenile court,
Nig was saved from a working-boys' institution
By the lies of his mother.
The tenement house that sheltered them
Had been condemned several years ago
As unfit for human beings.

Nig's boon companions were street wanderers like himself.
The slums had hardened them,
Sharpened their cunning,
Made them rapacious like wharf rats.

Nig was the leader of the Six Aces:
Petty thieves, crapshooters, and girl chasers,
Adroit in fishing things
From the wagons of hucksters and the counters of shops.
Eight times, with impunity,
Nig had snatched the pocketbooks of pedestrians.

At night the Six Aces met overwise girls
From the unchaste sidewalks of Harlem.
With Nig's skeleton key,

They entered unrented apartments
Where they ate sandwiches and drank hooch,
Told filthy jokes and indulged in bizarre lovemaking.

The Seven Black Dots
Were the chief rivals
Of the Six Aces,
And the two gangs fought many battles.

Late one afternoon,
During a blackjack game,
Nig was stabbed by Rip Waller
Of the Seven Black Dots.

9

For a week Nig held to life
By a slender thread.
Then, one night, while his mother was at the market,
A blaze started in the basement of the tenement house
And Nig was burned to death.

The Harlem Advocate carried the headline:
"Mayor Criticizes Courts For Permitting Old-Type Tenements!"

Abraham Dumas

An elderly man of catholic tastes and interests,
Nurtured by the cultures of two continents,
The Harlem Renaissance thrilled him
As an oasis makes tremulous a famished pilgrim.

He became the Flaubert
Of fledgling Negro poets and novelists,
Fathering them
With constructive criticism,
Interpreting their works
For white and for colored readers,
And introducing them
To unbiased editors and publishers.

Time and scholarship had mellowed his style, his judgments,
Like fine-grained wood seasoned for a costly instrument.
He was called "The Dean of Negro Letters."

One saw him going buoyantly about Harlem,
A little mustached man with the aspect of a Frenchman,
Gifted in polemics, sparkling in conversation,
Artistic to the polished tips of his fingers,
Full of hope and faith and charity.

Sometimes he withdrew into his dark tower,
Sat brooding over the crossword puzzle of events,
His eyes the eyes of the eternal mystic.
He seemed to be waiting for the coming of someone—
Perhaps . . . a black Whitman . . . a Balzac . . . a Tolstoi.

10

Deacon Phineas Bloom

Deacon Phineas Bloom lay on his deathbed
Groaning and tossing continually.
Mt. Sinai Baptist Church was gloomed with sorrow,
For the good man had worshipped there
During twenty-five, dramatic, soul-stirring years.

And now the Reverend Silas Grimstead
And Deaconess Isabella,
Wearing her small black bonnet
Trimmed with white linen,
And Sarah, the grief-torn wife,
Were kneeling in the bedroom of the dying man.

In that mornin', in that mornin',
When you face the Jedgment Seat,
Gawd will look into yo' record in that mornin'.

The pastor finished a long, eloquent prayer
In which he reminded God
Of the multitudinous virtues
Of Deacon Phineas Bloom
And asked for the divine guidance of his spirit
Into the Kingdom.

But Sarah wailed and wailed:
"O Gawd, if it is Thy will,
Spare ma faithful husband."

Deacon Phineas Bloom groaned piteously
And Deaconess Isabella,
Breathing words of comfort and of courage,
Placed a plump yellow arm
About the shoulders of the distressed wife.

Suddenly Deacon Phineas Bloom sat bolt upright
And cried in great agony of spirit:
"Sarah, forgive me befo' I face the Jedgment Seat!
Ma soul . . . it is tormented . . . Lawd."

The Reverend Silas Grimstead, his full red lips agape,
His eyes dilated with painful astonishment,
Swayed up to his gigantic height.
Sarah's skinny hands clutched at
Her shriveled and barren breasts.
Deaconess Isabella staggered toward the bed
And stretched a plump, protesting hand
Toward the wild, spectral figure
Shaped darkly against the snowy sheets.

For a moment the onlookers held their postures
Like ill-designed grotesques;
Then into the dusk and the silence
Dropped the naked confession of Deacon Phineas Bloom:
"Sarah, for these ten years I've committed adultery
With Deaconess Isabella. . . . O Sarah, ma wife,
Forgive me befo' I face the Jedgment Seat!"

Aunt Tommiezene

Face like an unclean coconut,
Eyes bleared with rheum,
Her body bowed like a hoop on an ancient sugar barrel,
Aunt Tommiezene,
Whose husband was tomahawked on the old Santa Fe Trail,
Stopped before the window of the Harlem Shoe Shop.

The north wind lashed around the corner of Eighth Avenue,
Whipping the old woman's shabby garments
Into a dissonance of rags,
Revealing the patched cotton stockings and the dilapidated shoes.

She peered into the lighted window
With its array of fine foot covering.
That black pair with the broad toes
Was just what she wanted . . . and needed.
She lifted her feet at intervals
From the cold of the pavement.

Above her bandana flashed the legend of the Harlem Shoe Shop:
"For Comfort and Service Wear Haskin Shoes!"

Snugly clad pedestrians
Hurried . . . unnoticed . . . past the huddled figure.
A lumbering streetcar
Disgorged its passengers and swallowed others . . .
Each isolated and glutted with his own petty purpose.

With a crooked leathery hand,
Aunt Tommiezene drew closer about her wasted body
The remains of the army jacket worn by her only son
Before the terrible malady contracted at Verdun
Ended his lagging death.

"For Comfort and Service Wear Haskin Shoes!"

You got shoes, I got shoes,
All Gawd's chillun got shoes.
When I git to hebben
Gonna put on ma shoes
An' walk all ovah Gawd's hebben.

The skeleton of a woman
Quaked with a violent fit of coughing.
Wearily she turned away from the lighted window
As a lady in a Russian sable coat
Paused and entered the Harlem Shoe Shop.

"For Comfort and Service Wear Haskin Shoes!"

Aunt Tommiezene hobbled around the street corner,
The north wind whipping her shabby garments
Into a dissonance of rags,
Revealing the patched cotton stockings and the dilapidated shoes.

Reverend Thomas Brazeale

His baritone voice reverberates
Through the capacious temple,
Like thunder leaping from crag to crag.
Infernal images zigzag
Through the cavern of his brain,
Like splinters of fractured light.
Beneath the overhanging brows
The expanding black eyes glow,
Like avid coals of fire.

An ebony Orpheus,
He plays upon the lyre of their emotions.
Leaning over the pulpit,
He draws the congregation forward in their pews,
Like a magnet tensing iron filings.

"Sinner, O Sinner, in the Last Judgment,
The wrath of an angry God
Will tear you limb from limb,
Like the grinding jaws of a starved lion!"

The temple shudders.
Glutted with fear,
Some shrink in their seats.
Some bound from their pews,
Like stricken deer.
Some grow taut
In grotesque attitudes.
Others hide their ashen faces in their hands
To shut out the awful picture.

But the vast majority,
Catching the mighty rhythms of the intoned periods,
Rock their bodies and stamp their feet.

Suddenly the man of God changes his manner:
The solid clouds of the Last Judgment
Break into thin fragments and vanish,
And the sun of peace glorifies the firmament.

His voice grows soothing like a mammy's lullaby.
The New Jerusalem appears,
And the cherubim and seraphim about the throne of God,
And the prophets that John the Revelator saw,

And the gold-paved avenues lighted with the radiance of God,
And the pearly gates opening on their diamond-studded hinges,
And the legions of the saved entering the Kingdom,
And the heavenly choir singing joyous anthems!

Exhausted,
The Reverend Thomas Brazeale takes his seat
In the midst of a crescendo of amens.
Professor Dos Passos launches the congregation
Into a militant and triumphant spiritual
That sets the temple resounding.

Senola Hurse

Senola Hurse has entered
One of Father Divine's heavens in Black Manhattan.
As one of the little dark God's angels,
She has forgotten the tragedies
on Federal Street in Chicago. . . .

Senola and Silas brought their son and daughter
From a jungle in the Mississippi Delta
To a shotgun shack on the South Side.

When Silas was earning good money in the stockyards,
Senola wanted him to take his family from that district
Of saloons, buffet flats, disorderly houses, and railroad tracks.

But the rent was cheap,
And Silas wanted to save money. Pinching his wife's chin,
Silas grinned: "Money is powah, Honey."
Senola nagged and nagged; her husband laughed.
The children grew larger . . . and harder.

The years trotted by.
One day Senola said: "I believe you's a misah, Silas."
He caught his breath . . . then chuckled and pinched her chin.
As the boy was crossing the tracks, drunk, one night,
He was killed by a switch engine.
The day before Silas was gored to death
By a mad bull in the stockyards,
His daughter ran off with a crapshooter from Montreal.

In one of Father Divine's heavens in Black Manhattan,
Senola is a dark angel singing: "Peace! Peace! I've found peace!"

16

Sootie Joe

The years had rubbed out his youth,
But his fellows ranked him still
As a chimney sweep without a peer . . .
Whether he raced a weighted corset
Up and down the throat of a freakish flue,
Or, from a chair of rope,
His eyes goggled and his mouth veiled,
He wielded his scraping knife
Through the walled-in darkness.

The soot from ancient chimneys
Had wormed itself into his face and hands.
The four winds had belabored the grime on him.
The sun had trifled with his ebony skin
And left ashen spots.

Sometimes Sootie Joe's wealthy customers
Heard him singing a song that gave them pause:

I's a chimney sweeper, a chimney sweeper,
I's black as the blackest night.
I's a chimney sweeper, a chimney sweeper,
And the world don't treat me right.
But somebody hasta black hisself
For somebody else to stay white.

Fritz Rickman

The scar Fritz Rickman received
The night Ku Klux riders
Drove all the Negroes out of Salem, Missouri,
Still shows on the back of his head.

He remembers the hooded figures in his bedroom,
The curses and threats and vulgarities,
The cold muzzle of a forty-four jammed against his temple.
He remembers harassed fugitives
Hurrying along rutty streets
With sacks and baskets and bundles . . .
The cries and whimpers of little children . . .
The collapse from heart failure of Uncle Jake,
Who loved his good white folk.
He remembers the honking cars and galloping horses
And the brutal curses to move on.
He remembers the daggers of pain ripping through his brain
And his mind becoming blacker than Salem. . . .

He awoke one morning in a rooming house,
Amazed at his surroundings . . . his strange surroundings,
He ran downstairs and asked the landlady where he was.
"On 135th Street in Harlem," she informed him quizzically.
He wondered: "How in the name of God did I get here?"

Yes . . . he was from Salem, Missouri, all right.
"Salem?" echoed Sister Slemp,
Thinking of *The Harlem Advocate*. Fear bulged her eyes.
"Mistah Ripley, ain't dat de place
Where de white folks mobbed po' Fritz Rickman?"

18

Sadie Mulberry

The Sunday morning that Reverend Graves
Welcomed Sadie Mulberry into the fellowship
Of Mt. Pisgah Baptist Church
Is still a red-letter day.

Sadie was the illegitimate daughter
Of Willa Mae Mulberry,
Who served many years as organist at Mt. Pisgah.
Sadie was the most notorious woman in Harlem.
She was dubbed "The Bootleg Queen."
Her brazen gowns and blazing diamonds and sinful escapades
Were the talk of Nigger Heaven.

No wonder Ma Goodwin almost died of heart failure
When Sadie, weeping bitterly for her sins, groped down the aisle!
Gone was the shimmy in her walk.
Gone was the form-revealing gown that enticed strong men.
Gone were the diamonds of the devil.

The Holy Ghost spread its wings over Mt. Pisgah,
And the various factions forgot their enmities
In the stormy ecstasy that almost wrecked the church.

Reverend Graves burst into a paroxysm of joy
And fell, sobbing, upon the collection table.
He had kept the secret promise made to Willa Mae Mulberry
As she lay dying in the Harlem Hospital.
With the help of God,
He had saved Sadie Mulberry . . . "The Bootleg Queen" . . .
His own daughter!

Biffo Lightfoote

Biffo Lightfoote had an eye for business
When he opened The Chicken Shack,
Two doors from the Harlem Opera House,
Where the theater crowds could see in big electric lights:

"The Best Fried Chicken in Town"

"Black folks like chicken," said Mother Vibbard,
" 'Cause durin' slavery time
De white folks et all de best ov de chicken
An' give de niggers de feets an' necks an' gizzards.
I's been eatin' chicken foh nigh unto a hundred years,
An' Biffo Lightfoote cooks de best I's et."

The Chicken Shack was not a shack.
It was a well-appointed café,
With a fleet of delivery cars and uniformed drivers
Who would bring the delicacy right to your door.
Harlem celebrities, like Peg Leg Snelson, Big Bessie,
Napoleon Hannibal Speare, and Snakehips Flippen,
Dined in The Chicken Shack.

Biffo married Maebelle Haste
And then his troubles began.
Rumors said she was sweet-daddying with a Pullman porter,
But Biffo could never catch her with the creeper.
One day a huge brown woman from Texarkana, Texas,
Strode into The Chicken Shack with a Jewish policeman.
Biffo Lightfoote is in jail on a charge of bigamy.

20

Lady Hope

Lady Hope was an octoroon from Lake Charles, Louisiana.
Her first serious mistake in life
Was her marriage to Rex Gollomb,
Who was near-white and handsome and stiff-necked.
He whiled away most of his time
In the basement poolroom of Tony the Greek,
Or in consoling the misunderstood wives
Of henpecked Sugar Hill businessmen.

Finally, in disgust and desperation,
Lady Hope divorced Gollomb and married Sam Childs,
Who was black and ugly and well-to-do,
A man who would appreciate a high yellow woman.

For two years Lady Hope was unbelievably happy:
Each week Sam gave her the earnings from his modest store
And slavishly courted her ivory whiteness.

Precipitately
Sam fell in love with Black Zuleika,
Who danced the Jelly Roll and sang the *Yellah Gal Blues*
In the Sundown Cabaret on Upper Lenox Avenue.

Her gold teeth shining in twin rows,
Her lean-muscled body swaying like a tall palm
Caught in a simoom, Black Zuleika sang huskily:
Look out, Yellah Gal, look out!
Bettah tie yo' man at home,
'Cause I got the kind ov lovin'
That makès the men-folks roam!

Black Zuleika

Black Zuleika boasted that her lovers
Had come from the four corners of the earth
And twenty different nationalities.
She had not counted them beyond the ninety-ninth,
A tattooed Javanese sailor,
Since ninety-nine was her lucky number.

Down at Onward, Mississippi, ten years ago,
A yellow field girl had stolen her peon-husband,
And Black Zuleika had sworn vengeance
On the whole race of yellow women.

Not even the unstinted tips her covetous fingers received
From hilarious patrons in the Sundown
Delighted Black Zuleika half so much
As a liaison with a yellow woman's husband.

Marcus Quest had composed the *Yellah Gal Blues*
As a tribute to Black Zuleika's glamorous notoriety,
And the blues-ballad had led Harlem captive.
In dim apartments dancers rocked to the song,
In cheap theaters orchestras blared the song,
In alleyways overbold children chanted the song.

One night Marcus Quest sat in the Sundown Cabaret,
His passionate eyes devouring the thighs of the blues singer . . .
And the next morning he slipped noiselessly out
Of Black Zuleika's loud-red bedroom
And went home to his yellow wife
With an oily lie on the tip of his tongue.

Babe Quest

When Sam Childs told Babe that her husband
Had stayed all night with Black Zuleika,
Babe sat on the edge of the divan
Like an ill-boding statue made of yellow clay.

I love ma daddy,
But ma daddy's been untrue.
Love ma daddy,
But ma daddy's been untrue.
Ma daddy hurt me so bad
I don't know what to do.

The woman's unavoidable eyes grilled Sam Childs.
The copious yellow lips drew into a menacing line.
Sam became fidgety and wiped his ashy-blue mouth
With the back of his slender hand.

A low, broken whimper filled the bleak room.
Sam Childs mumbled and moved toward the door.
Trembling uncontrollably,
He fussed with the knob
And stumbled into the hallway,
Dropping his twisted hat.

Babe got up stiffly . . .
Like one in a trance . . .
Put on her coat,
And walked downstairs.

She went straight to old Goldberg's pawnshop
And sullenly bargained with him for a razor.
Weighing a question in his mind,
Old Goldberg, beetle-browed,
Watched the woman run her thumb along the blade,
An inhuman glow in the slits of her eyes.

The old Jew shrugged his shoulders
As the woman entered the street. . . .

23

Down at Onward, Mississippi,
The Reverend Elijah Brand,
Amid the weeping of Black Zuleika's relatives and friends,
Looked upon the cheap coffin before the altar,
Adjusted his brass-rimmed glasses,
And said in a voice of infinite sadness:
"Brothahs an' sistahs, de wages ov sin is death."

Francis Keats

I have known futility,
The desolate servitude of language,
The vanity of trying to put into words
The things I have felt.

Aboard the *Scorpion*
In the soggy midnight of the Sulu Sea
I saw a typhoon streak, like a Limited from Hell,
And crash into our greasy freighter with mountains of water.

On an Ozark crag
Years and years ago
I heard the almost-human whimper of a lost dog
In the straining coils of a huge snake.

In the Mississippi evening
On the veranda of an antebellum Big House
I heard the stirring protest of an age-old worksong
Drifting across a snowy ocean of cotton.

On a California mountainside
With the tranquil stars as witnesses
I saw a blonde woman set fire to the oil-soaked victim
Whose crazed laughter was lost in the carnival shouts of the mob.

I have known futility,
The desolate servitude of language,
The vanity of trying to put into words
The things I have felt.

24

Grand Chancellor Knapp Sackville

In his flashy blue uniform,
With his breast glittering with self-awarded medals,
And his great embellished sword clanking,
And his yellow plume tossing like a horse's mane,
And his black boots shining like metallic mirrors in the sun . . .
Mr. Knapp Sackville,
Grand Chancellor and Most Exalted Polemarch
Of the Sons and Daughters of Ethiopia,
Cut a magniloquent figure in the Capital of the Negro World.

His pride of race overflowed
Like a plugged bathtub.
Race efficiency and race unity
Flashed through his speeches
Like blinking lights on a billboard at midnight.

Money-making was his religion
And the Jewish businessman his god.
"Look at the Jew!" he cried,
Storming up and down the platform in Liberty Hall.
"White folks don't like Jews,
But the Jews' money commands respect!
Negroes must stop being like crabs!
Negroes must organize!
Negroes must pool their money!
Negroes must boycott foreigners!
Negroes must buy where they can work!
Negroes must buy from Negro businesses!"

Grand Chancellor Knapp Sackville organized
The One Hundred Per Cent Negro Club,
Carried his campaign into the Harlem churches,
Flashed slogans on the screens of moving-picture houses,
Paid small boys to carry placards through the streets,
Cursed his easy-going people,
And averred he was a black John the Baptist
Crying in the Harlem wilderness!

Editor Crum

For fifty years
Editor Crum has published *The Bingham Star*.
His father, who was with Lee at Appomattox Courthouse,
Had been the largest slaveholder in Clay County, Georgia.
On his plantation had lived Mammy Suhrie,
Who nursed Bingham's most distinguished citizen.

Whenever Editor Crum talks about Mammy Suhrie,
His eyes become misty and his nose watery.
Only a good draught of Old Hickory tranquilizes him then.
Editor Crum always carries his bottle on his hip
And votes for Temperance.
"Gen'lemen, niggers an' white trash can't drink like gen'lemen.
Liquor makes 'em hot in the tail."

Mammy Suhrie is living in Harlem with her grandnephew,
And Editor Crum visits her once a year
When business brings him North.

"Gen'lemen," effervesces Editor Crum, "I love Mammy Suhrie,
An' I'll kill any bastard who touches a hair on her head!"
When he visits her,
He leaves a hundred dollars on her lap.

Niggers would be all right
If it wasn't for these damn Yankees
Putting social equality into their skulls.
"Nobody loves niggers better than me, Gen'lemen,
When they stay in their place like Mammy Suhrie."

He had paid Mammy Suhrie a visit.
A black cop stopped him on Seventh Avenue
When his Ford ran past a red light.
Bingham doesn't have traffic signals.
And if the town did,
What would it matter to Editor Crum?

The black cop said:
"What's wrong with your brakes?"
That made Editor Crum as mad as hell.
The uppity nigger talking to Mr. Crum like that!
Red in the face, the gentleman snorted:
"If I had you in Bingham, Georgia. . . ."

The jaws of the black cop grew tight
Like the head of a drum. His eyes blazed.
"Get that rattletrap to the curb," he sharped.
"You're not in Bingham, Georgia. See?"

Anger almost suffocated Editor Crum.
His purple lips twitched.
He was thinking: "O God, if I had my forty-four,
I'd kill this black sonofabitch!"

Editor Crum paid his fine,
And when he returned to Bingham, Georgia,
He wrote a series of violent articles
On "The Black Peril" and "The Decline of Caucasian Civilization."

Stillicho Spikes

The scuffed walls of tenements
Towered on either hand
Like the aeon-drubbed sides of a Colorado canyon.

In the scurvy streets
The heat waves danced
Like wraiths from a stagnant river.

Stripped to the waist,
His muscles gnarled like ebony cord,
Stillicho swung his mighty pick
As the ballad of his dusky Ulysses
Climbed the perpendicular tenements:

John Henry said if you give me a drink
I'll finish dis job befo' a cat kin wink.
When Gawd made me, He made a man
Who's de best steel-driver in all de lan'.

The sweat rolled down Stillicho's body,
And the sweat rolled down his face,
And the blurs of objects wavered before his eyes.

He wiped his face with a soggy rag.
The rise and fall of the curving pick
Matched the rhythm of his song:

John Henry worked in all kinds ov weather . . .
'Cause a workin' man cain't do no better.

Stillicho dreamed of his small son
And the new suit he would buy the lad
When he was graduated from the high school . . .
The first Spikes to get a diploma.
The boy was smart.
The white principal expected great things of him.
Perhaps he'd be a second Booker T.
The thought made the pick rise and fall
Like the regal stick of a drum major.

John Henry he had a little boy,
An' he was John Henry's pride an' joy.
John Henry said he'll make a man
As good as any in dis wide, wide lan'.

Stillicho thought of his wife
And the big pot of cabbage and ham hock
She was cooking for his dinner.

He saw the pride shining in her eyes
When he brought his check home on a Saturday night
And hid it where she could find it.

Stillicho looked at the slanting sun.
He spat on his horny hands and rubbed them and grinned.

John Henry he had a pretty wife,
An' her name it was Polly Ann.
She loved her home an' she loved her kid
An' she loved her steel-drivin' man.

Peg Leg Snelson

Peg Leg Snelson
Is strutting his stuff at the Harlem Club.
I saw him stop the show on Broadway
In the *Dark Town Scandals of 1929*.
He can tap out the intricate rhythms
Of seventeen routines,
Including the Staircase Shuffle and the Delta Stomp.
He has taught three or four white actors in Hollywood.

Snelson lost his left leg in Houston, Texas,
When a truckload of white strikebreakers
Crashed into a Ford containing
Six Negro longshoremen.

Heart's so heavy cain't raise a song,
Heart's so heavy cain't raise a song,
Gonna catch de first train comin' along.

Mr. Heinrich Zangwill discovered Peg Leg Snelson
At a cheap beer garden on Market Street in St. Louis. . . .

Peg Leg Snelson has now
Fifty vivid suits and six high yellow women
And a high-powered roadster.
His wild parties in his Sugar Hill apartment
Cause the preachers to denounce him.
He tips often and he tips big.
He bets on everything . . . everything . . .
From a bedbug race in a honky-tonk
To his ability to make a deacon's wife the first night.

Frederick Judson

Frederick worked in the drying room
Of a Virginian tobacco factory.
Captain Osgood, his master, was the descendant
Of a long line of rich planters
Whose forbears had come from Devonshire
And settled at Jamestown in the seventeenth century.

The master was a God-fearing man
Who did not whip his slaves himself
And permitted no other man to do so.
Once an English overseer kicked Captain Osgood's valet,
And the master felled the Englishman
With one blow of his famous fist.

Just before Captain Osgood died,
He set all his slaves free
And gave each man and each woman twenty acres.

Frederick sold his land at a good price
And worked his way on a ship to New York.
He rented a small shop and became a cigar maker.
He knew all grades of tobacco,
And he was expert, conscientious, and courteous.
In a short time he built up a thriving business
Among the old aristocrats of the city.
Frederick's ideas were those of the master class:
He scorned both the poor whites and the poor blacks.

To this day he boasts of the compliment
Passed by General Grant
As he stood in the tobacco shop
With a Chicago railroad magnate.

"It's an honor to make a cigar like this,"
Said the ex-businessman from Galena, Illinois.

Frederick always takes out-of-town visitors
To the tomb of Ulysses Grant
Hard by the romantic Hudson.

While they gaze down,
A little awed,
Upon his hero's imposing mausoleum,
Frederick shakes his head sadly and muses:
"Here lies the noblest general of them all."

Frederick Judson is a venerable citizen of Harlem,
An officer in the highbrow St. John's Episcopal Church,
And a favorite among the young folk of the Dark Four Hundred.

He likes to talk about the Negro's will to survive.
"My people will make it, somehow," he triumphs.
"I've seen them come through darker days than these."

Chittling Sue

On Central Avenue in Los Angeles
Chittling Sue's mother supported the family
By washing and ironing for the white folk.
With a dope-using husband who couldn't hold a job
And her children going to the dogs
Because she didn't have time to take care of them,
The mother became desperate.

One quiet Sunday after the church services
She served the family a big chicken dinner,
And Chittling Sue was the only one
Who didn't die of poisoning.

Grief-stricken for months,
The girl decided to go as far away as possible
From the haunted house on Central Avenue.
So she crossed the continent to Harlem
And went to work at a hole-in-the-wall restaurant.

When the Greek went out of business
Sue took over the place,
And it wasn't long before her chittlings
Became the talk of Lenox Avenue.
The black folk came from all parts of Harlem,
And the white folk followed.

If you haven't eaten in the Chittling Palace,
You've missed one of the delights of life.
Chittling Sue has five apartment houses on Strivers' Row.

Harlem Big Shots, like Grand Chancellor Knapp Sackville,
Come to her to get the lowdown on business.
The little Greek is one of her cooks, when he isn't dead drunk.
And she pays him well.

But Harlem wants to know why Chittling Sue
Never goes to church,
Never attends a party,
Never has a sweet daddy,
Never visits anybody.

Brother Hester says
She's the same Chittling Sue
Who used to serve him
At the little Greek's hole-in-the-wall.

Doc Brockenbury

Along Eighth Avenue any of the ancients will tell you
Doc Brockenbury was a man of his word.

He loved his dingy little drugstore
Better than his dingy little wife.

From the street you could see him
In his stiffly starched white jacket,
Sitting behind the decrepit showcase,
Smoking his obnoxious brier-root pipe.

When he placed a customer's money
In his companionable cash register
And religiously closed the drawer,
His face became almost human.

Then his pharmacy was held up
Twice in twelve days.

Over the protests of his wife,
Doc pocketed his revolver
And swore he'd never be robbed again.

Before closing for the night,
Doc was counting the money in the cash register.
Sty Tears, who had lost heavily in The Greasy Spoon,
Entered and asked for a package of cigarettes.
As Doc shuffled toward the tobacco showcase,
Sty Tears snapped: "Stick 'em up!"

Doc reached for his revolver
As three shots rang out.
Seized by a sudden, overpowering fear,
Sty Tears backed away,
Dropping his thirty-eight.

With a tremendous effort
That tore a blood-vessel,
Doc pulled himself to his feet
And fired at the cowering figure.

It crumpled like an empty bag
At the feet of Officer Bill Shanks,
Who stepped through the door at the moment.

Along Eighth Avenue the ancients will tell you
Doc Brockenbury was a man of his word.

Poker Face Duncan

Does you roll de bones?
Does you play de stocks?
You's a gambler anyway.
If you win or lose
In dis White Man's Land,
You got to pay an' pay.

When Poker Face Duncan pocketed the last billiard ball
With an extraordinary shot
That won a fat bet from Slim Hayes,
The cavernous Deep Ditch became blatant with praise.

Poker Face glanced at Slim,
Beyond the green-coned droplight,
And read in Slim's cat-gray eyes
The sinister message he'd seen from coast to coast
And from the Gulf to the Great Lakes
In the eyes of desperate losers.

Slim's facile fingers slipped into his hip pocket
And came out with a Dallas Special.

At the other end of the billiard table
Poker Face Duncan stood
Chewing a wad of gum.

Slim Hayes pressed the tiny spring:
A silvery click punctuated the silence with a period
As the gleaming blade traced a portentous arc.

Slim measured his man and moved forward,
Crouching,
The murder-hunger luminous in his eyes.
His figure shaped itself,
Like an arabesque question mark,
Upon the illuminated billiard table.

The speech-deserted onlookers
Slunk into the ashen shadows
And gazed at the miniature drama . . . fascinated.

Like a plummet,
The hand of Poker Face Duncan
Dropped into a pocket of the billiard table;
And then,
Quicker than the naked eye could follow the arched movement,
An underhand swing of the arm
Sent the ivory ball through the air.

Slim Hayes pitched forward
Upon his face . . .
And lay quite still.

Sarah Ashton

Christmas is a time fer wishin' . . .
An' I wish ma chillen had never been borned.
.I been sufferin' in this low ground of sorrow
Ever since they got any size. I been alone.

De sun don't shine no mo', ma Lawd,
De sun don't shine no mo'.
Ma mother's gone to Glory, Lawd,
An' now I wants to go.

Ma daughter kept runnin' round
With Ferenc Glaspell . . .
That no-'count porter at the Harlem Hotel . . .
Till he filled her full of babies.
Then Uncle Sam drafted 'im to the army
An' we ain't heard nothin' an' seen nothin' of him since.
I wanted ma daughter to be a teacher.
I worked like a truck-horse to make somethin' outa her.
Lawdy . . . Lawdy . . . Lawdy . . .
Sometimes I sees her solicitin' on Lenox Avenue!

There is ma son, Joel.
I wanted 'im to be a doctor . . . like Dr. Harvey Whyte.
Joel is in Sing Sing now,
Fer breakin' into a jewelry store an' killin' Mr. Absalom.
Joel had been stealin' all his life.
It was bred in his bones by his father, I guess.
Christmas is a time fer wishin' . . .
An' I wish ma chillen had never been borned.

36

Daddy Oldfield

An ole stud feels he's in his prime
An' daddies gay young mares.
An ole man fiddlin' pretty gals
Don't give a damn who cares.

Daddy Oldfield married
That gay young widow, Ida Bibbs,
Before Sarah's body
Had settled in the cold, cold grave.

This unwonted flouting of respectability
Rocked Galilee Baptist Church
To its ancient foundation.

Wives who feared the evil effect
Of Daddy Oldfield's example
Paraded the domestic virtues and sacrifices
Of the deceased wife
In the presence of husbands sick of marital woes.

Hettie Sprigg,
Jealous because the deacon had not made love to her,
Said to her pastor one evening:
"Reveren' Greene,
You shouldn't have let de ole fool
Stage dat big weddin' in de house of Gawd.
It was a sin an' a shame . . .
A sin an' a shame."

Bud Daddy Oldfield,
Gaudily dressed like a Harlem sweet man,
Strutted down the middle aisle the very next Sunday
And directed Ida to the very pew
Where Sarah Oldfield had worshipped for thirty years.

Seeing Ida's fleshy hips,
Brazenly outlined,
Shimmying under her flaming red dress
And her voluptuous breasts
Trembling like plump apples on a wind-stirred bough . . .
The eyes of the sisters flashed righteous indignation.

Six days later
The scandalous news was noised about

That Daddy Oldfield had been found
Doubled up in bed,
Holding his lower stomach
Just as he had died.

Hettie Sprigg lingered on the church steps
After the funeral services.
Thinking of Ida's shimmying hips and voluptuous breasts,
She smiled evilly and said to Mother Vibbard:
"An ole fool can commit suicide in mo' ways
Dan by hangin' hisself."

Margaret Levy

My wife was the soprano soloist
At the highbrow St. John's Episcopal Church.

We received a gold-edged invitation
To the dance of the Sugar Hill Aristocrats.
Margaret wanted a new evening gown.
But how could I buy anything
With bill collectors on my doorsteps
Like buzzards around a carcass?

Margaret said tearfully:
"John, I'm going through that door
And I'm never coming back.
I'm sick of cabbage and bacon.
I'm tired of making old dresses over.
I'm tired of cooking and washing and cleaning house.
I'm a woman. I want to live . . .
To travel . . . to do things . . . to be somebody."

I saw her put on her little hat
And walk into the night of 137th Street . . . saw her walk
Out of my life forever.

I couldn't say a word . . . a mumbling word.
My wife was the soprano soloist at a highbrow church,
But I heard her voice in a vast chorus . . .
A chorus of millions and millions
Of overworked, underfed, poorly clad women
Singing the "Hard Luck Blues" in the Land of Plenty!

Jacob Nollen

Troubled waters, troubled waters,
Done begin to roll.
Troubled waters, troubled waters,
Gittin' deep an' col'.
Lawd, don't let dem troubled waters
Drown ma weary soul!

All the way home
Jacob sat brooding in the subway train . . .
A ragged Negro scratched his buttocks and dozed beside him,
A sleek Japanese in a corner seat dreamed of Manchuria,
A stout Irish woman read a lurid scandal sheet,
An opium-stinking Chinese glared at the Japanese,
A pock-marked American read the baseball news and chuckled,
A Jewish rabbi looked mournfully at the rag of a Negro . . .
All the way home
Jacob sat brooding in the subway train.

Troubled waters, troubled waters,
Done begin to roll.
Troubled waters, troubled waters,
Gittin' deep an' col'.
Lawd, don't let dem troubled waters
Drown ma weary soul.

Miss Felicia Babcock

Miss Felicia Babcock, on a slumming trip to Harlem,
Discovered that Negroes are delightful children,
Primitive children,
Irresponsible children;
And the old lady's wonder exceeded her favorite poet's
On first looking into Chapman's Homer.

Her fugitive spirit found a city of refuge
In the Renaissance of Negro Art:
She opened her salon to the Harlem intelligentsia,
Established the Babcock Exhibition of African Cultures,
And granted the Annual Babcock Awards in Negro Art.

Critics and writers and YMCA workers from Harlem
Sipped the good lady's champagne from crystalline glasses
And tickled her delicate ears with paeans.
Inspired by a bottle of Burgundy,
Which his doting patron had slipped into his overcoat pocket,
Young Marc Comstock celebrated her in a sparkling sonnet
As the polestar in the Renaissance of Negro Art.

Miss Felicia Babcock's white friends were shocked
To find her spacious chambers adorned with
Fetish figures from the Banagala tribe,
Wooden drinking cups from the Bena Lulua,
Huge head-shield masks from the Kundu,
Ivory statuettes from the Wazimba,
Mortuary figures from the Bakuni,
And colossal snuffboxes of beaten gold from the Badjok kings.

Pictures of the gracious lady
Seated among African works of art
Appeared in the metropolitan feature magazines;
And many strangers came to see her,
Among them a bespectacled Western professor
Who handled the bizarre objects with reverential fingers
And talked in hushed tones about lost African civilizations
Of which Miss Felicia Babcock had never heard.

The old lady was happy . . .
Happier than she had ever dreamed of being;
And, despite the protests of her dear white friends,
She voyaged, like some bold Elizabethan explorer,
To the Gold Coast
To collect other rare specimens. . . .
While there she died of blackwater fever.

Miss Felicia Babcock was placed . . .
As she had planned . . .
In an ebony coffin
Ornamented with polished African ivory,
With the figures of two African witch doctors
At her head
And two at her feet.

Many things are lost in the flux of the years,
But the image of the old lady
In her brocaded silks
Remains with her Harlem friends.

41

Grandma Lonigan

Gawd sent dis depression. Don't fergit dat, Chile.
He sent it to teach de white folks a lesson,
Jest as He let down de seven plagues on Egypt.

You know, Chile, when a people is ridin' high,
Dey fergits all about de Lawd Gawd Jehovah.
Dey gits puffed up an' beside deyself
An' go struttin' about like a peacock.

But don't de Good Book say somewheres,
"Pride goeth before a great fall"?
I ain't never read it,
But I's heard ole Reveren' Joshua Battles
Preach on dat text at Mt. Carmel
Off an' on fer pretty nigh twenty years,
An' what ole Reveren' Joshua Battles says
Comes from de Lawd Gawd Jehovah hisself.

De white folks is right down in de breadlines now
Where we poor black folks has been all our lives.
Hereintofore, we's been doin' all de sqawkin' about injustice;
Now de white folks is sqawkin'.
Chile, hungry dawgs all acts alike . . .
An' dawgs with cropped tails knows how it feels. Yes, Lawd!

Miss Sherrill says to me as I hangs up clothes yistidday:
"Grandma Lonigan, dis depression is terrible. What'll we do?"
I says to her: "Keep on inchin' along, Miss Sherrill.
You see us black folks was borned in a depression;
So we inches along with de help of de Lawd Gawd Jehovah."

Sister Slemp

High yellah woman is like de angels above,
High yellah woman is like de angels above;
Give me a chocolate gal when it comes to love.

Sister Slemp,
Barrellike, forbidding,
Darker than the surrounding night,
Stood at the front window
In a short, cotton nightgown.

One of her fantastic plaits
Struck the cretonne curtain
As she pulled it aside stealthily
To observe the couple standing on the shadowy stoop.

She saw Noble Fetchit,
Who hadn't paid for his board and room in seven weeks,
Catch the chocolate-colored girl in his sinewy arms
And fiercely press her plump body to him.

Sister Slemp sighed a desolate sigh
As she put a fleshy hand absent-mindedly to her vast bosom
Where an imp of jealousy goaded her heart.

Then she heard the door open cautiously
And worldly-wise steps ascending the ancient stairs.
Came a woman's strained whisper
And a waggish warning from Noble Fetchit
To avoid the eleventh stair . . . which creaked.
A spasm of anger seized Sister Slemp,
And she restrained herself with an Amazonian effort.

Her mind tormented by lustful imaginings,
She put on her voluminous kimono
And waddled up to the second floor.
Oblivious of the cold December night,
She groped down the unlighted hallway,
The passkey shaking in her hand.

43

The interminable journey ended,
She placed her ear against the door . . . and listened . . .
Big drops of sweat
Oozing down the ugly crag of her face.
Came the amorous whimpering of the chocolate-colored girl;
And Sister Slemp,
Launching her barrellike body against the door,
Crashed into the dark room.

The frantic cry of the chocolate-colored girl
Split the night in twain.
"What the hell?"
A masculine voice challenged the intruder.

From all parts of the house
Roomers gathered in their agitated nightclothes,
Chattering like excited monkeys.

Sister Slemp blocked the doorway, screaming:
"Git dat lettle whoah outa ma house!
I ain't nevah had ma place disgraced befo' . . . .
Noble Fetchit, git dat lettle whoah outa ma house!"

44

Silhouettes

Hester Pringle

Hester came in from the weekly meeting
Of the Deaconess Purity League.
The minute book was still in her hand
When she opened the door to the bathroom
Which all the lodgers used in the old apartment house.

Hurriedly and shamefacedly
Hester closed the door,
For there in the bathtub stood Gus Matsner,
His bronze, hard-muscled body
Glistening with beads of water.
Hester let out a little cry
And dropped the minutes of the Deaconess Purity League.

> *When you's a-settin' at de table*
> *Eatin' cake an' chicken,*
> *How in de hell kin you tell*
> *What's hap'nin' in de kitchen?*

And in the days that followed
Tiny electric tremors raced through Hester
Whenever she passed Gus Matsner in the hallway;
And in the days that followed
Hester felt like a pilloried criminal
Whenever she wrote down the proceedings
Of the Deaconess Purity League;
And in the nights that followed
Hester saw herself naked,
Pursued in the moonlight of a tropical garden
By a bronze, hard-muscled body
Glistening with beads of water.

David Letts

Old David Letts sits in his creaking rocking chair,
Looking at his hands . . . looking at his hands . . .
Hands worn and cracked like the rusty leather apron
Ned Stearns, the blacksmith, used to wear
Down in Alabama.

When his wife gave birth to twin boys,
David promised her . . .
Before she sank into everlasting forgetfulness . . .
That he would make fine men of them.

Since he was afraid to marry again,
Afraid of a woman who might mistreat his sons,
David hired ancient Aunt Jenny . . .
Good-natured, painstaking Aunt Jenny . . .
To bring up the boys in the way they should go.

Meanwhile David tended his crops, his chickens, his hogs . . .
And saved his hard-earned dollars
To educate his sons.

And as they approached manhood's high estate,
Strong and straight-eyed and thrifty like their father,
David's bosom grew big with paternal pride.

Once he heard Booker T. speak
To a silent multitude on the courthouse square,
And David decided then
That Tuskegee was the place for his sons.

One hot afternoon
The boys went into town to trade,
Leaving David alone,
Hoeing in the cottonfield.

A thousand times
David has lived over that eternity of crucifixion
When Aunt Jenny ran crazily across the clayey furrows
Screaming to him the news
Of the lynching of his sons. . . .

48

Old David Letts sits in his creaking rocking chair,
Looking at his hands . . . looking at his hands . . .
Hands worn and cracked like the rusty leather apron
Ned Stearns, the blacksmith, used to wear
Down in Alabama.

Life has written old David's biography in his hands.

Rhoda Stacpoole

Rhoda keeps busy
Going up and down the hallways,
Listening at closed doors,
Peeping through keyholes,
And watching from her bathroom window
The families across the rear courtyard.

Rhoda keeps busy
Carrying spicy morsels of gossip
To sex-starved women in the neighborhood . . .
Women who abide her coming
Like fledglings
Awaiting the mother bird
With choice crumbs.

Rhoda keeps so busy,
Attending to other folks' business,
She does not see her ten-year-old daughter
Sneak into the unrented apartment next door
With overwise little black boys
From the unchaste sidewalks of Harlem.

Napoleon Hannibal Speare

Editor-in-chief and sole owner of *The Harlem Advocate*,
Defender of the Rights of Negro Citizens,
Napoleon Hannibal Speare dedicated his talents
To the abolition of race prejudice in the United States.

He was in the seventh heaven
When he could boast about the Negro's achievements,
Or see jealousy in the eyes of poor whites
As he rode through the country in his high-powered car.

Any Aframerican who squeezed through
A Caucasian university with his M.A.
Could get his picture
On the front page of *The Harlem Advocate*
And be exploited as an example
Of the equality of races.

And if the Aframerican could cram enough
To have his name embellished with a Ph.D.,
Beneath his imposing likeness would appear a panegyric
Indited by some Daniel Webster of Upper Lenox Avenue.

Napoleon Hannibal Speare was in great demand
As a commencement orator in the Bible Belt;
And, although his honorary degrees were legion,
They were spread in glittering array behind the name
Of the editor-in-chief and sole owner
Of the Negro's Greatest Weekly.

In his grandiloquent periods
Napoleon Hannibal Speare told his audiences
How he had worked his way up from a bootblack's stand
And that he was proud,
Proud to be black . . .
Proud that not a single drop of Caucasian blood
Flowed in his veins.

The black folk listened . . .
As black folk listen . . .
And exchanged glances
And snickered
And looked at the wife of Napoleon Hannibal Speare—
The wife who was as white as a Swede.

50

Pat Frost

Sister Slemp thinks the boy a criminal,
Because he can't look you in the eye
And his head has a doglike droop.

Years ago
In a seedy Missouri town,
Pat's father came home in a drunken rage
From the Last Chance Saloon
And horsewhipped the boy's mother.

Sheriff Mike Hardy
Drove his rattletrap Ford across the tracks into Frogtown
And arrested Caleb Frost.

The county bosses needed men
For the new road work . . .
Needed them badly.

"Have to teach you niggers in Frogtown a lesson,"
Philosophized His Honor,
As he sentenced Caleb to six months of hard labor.

When Caleb got out
He never held up his head again in Frogtown,
He never spoke to his wife again,
Nor to his son.

One evening he came in dog-weary,
Tossed some things into a battered suitcase,
And crossed the river on Daddy Jacobs's side-wheeler.

A terrible silence entered the weather-beaten house,
Its black arms embosoming
The frail woman and her son.

The housewives ate the crumbs of gossip
And wore their lives away on petty tasks.

One morning
After a violent storm
The boy went to his mother's bed
And called her
And touched her strangely cold shoulder.

She was buried
In the man-forsaken graveyard
Behind the Church of God.

51

Reverend Gould adopted the boy
And worked him like a galley slave on his stubbly farm
And beat him religiously
And frightened him with the terrors of hell.

In his nineteenth year
The boy ran off with a minstrel show.

He never speaks
Unless spoken to,
And his face is like an emptied black jar.
Sister Slemp thinks the boy a criminal,
Because he can't look you in the eye
And his head has a doglike droop.

Lovie Long

Lovie stood near the front of the stage,
Putting all her old tricks into the "Rocky Road Blues."
Her cleverness alone enabled her to hold her own
Against younger rivals with better voices.

Rocky Road Blues . . . Rocky Road Blues.
Men had passed in and out of Lovie's life
Like patrons in and out of the Harlem Theatre.

When a woman has traveled the tortuous route
From a shack down at Waycross, Georgia,
Snatched an hour of fame in a swank casino on the Riviera,
And descended to the shabby stage of the Harlem Theatre,
Her lips have known the reddest wines of pleasure
And the ashes of disillusion.

Rocky Road Blues . . . Rocky Road Blues.
Lovie looked down at the little bald-headed yellow man
Sitting on the front row in the middle aisle.

He had told his dark Xanthippe
He was going to a meeting of the Sons of Ethiopia.
He winked and grinned at the blues singer
And felt arrogantly masculine.
He had a midnight date with Lovie.

Sparky Zigsmith

Sparky sat smoking a reefer in the Harlem Theatre,
His polished shoes decking the tarnished rail
In the sepulchral gallery.

Too bad he had to kill that cop out in Cheyenne
When he held up that filling station last week!

The husky-voiced singer
Was wailing the "Rocky Road Blues."
The ballad raked desolate memories
Under Sparky's patent-leather hair.
He thought of little Iona,
Whom he had deserted an eternity ago
When her father had shot at him for ruining his daughter.

Where was Iona now?
What was she doing?
What had become of the baby?
Rocky Road Blues! Rocky Road Blues!
Sparky had traveled, too, a long treacherous road
Since he'd caught an outgoing freight
That night in a snarling snowstorm. . . .

What was his old man doing?
Still riding a Methodist circuit in Oklahoma?
The boy's sin had hurt old Reverend Zigsmith, all right.

The reefer butt burned Sparky's finger.
He dropped it . . . ground it under his leather heel.
Rocky Road Blues . . . Rocky Road Blues. . . .

Enloe Penn

He was pot-bellied and blear-witted,
With yellow teeth and a bullet head,
And the fumes of the last drink still clogged his brain.

He was sitting across from Sparky Zigsmith.
He was sitting beside Big Stiff,
The pal who had saved his life in a hobo jungle
Near Battle Creek, Michigan.
Enloe hiccoughed and said:

"Big Stiff, you see that little black gal
Dancin' on the extreme left of the line?
Well, she looks jest like that hot mama
I met at that dance in El Paso.

"I started dancin' with her, Big Stiff,
An' at the very first we fell for each other. See?
After we'd belly-rolled about three dances,
She started gittin' red hot
An' I felt my love comin' down. See?

"When we was beginnin' the fourth,
Up comes an ugly bastard. See?
He was bigger an' blacker than Jack Johnson. See?

"He puts his hands on his hips, squares his legs,
An' looks down on me . . . looks down on me
Like a gorilla lookin' down on a cornered monkey. See?
I acts indignant . . . Big Stiff . . . very indignant.
I says to him, superiorlike:
'Sir, why the ungen'lemanly conduct?'

"I sees I got his goat. So I turns to Venus—
That was the little black gal's name—
An' I says in a Fifth Avenue style:
'Miss Venus, may I escort you outa the obnoxious presence
Of such unbecomin' acquaintanceship?

54

In New Yawk,
Where I come from an' have my place of domicile,
I shot six men fer less than this.
Gawd knows I don't like to murder nobody!
But when a gen'leman is insulted, Miss Venus,
In the celestial presence
Of one of Gawd's fairest creatures,
What can a he-man do but murder a brute?'

"That nigger stood up there
Like he was seein' a miracle.
I could have knocked him down with a toothpick. See?
Venus was skeered to death.
I took her by the arm an' walked away,
While the niggers stood there gapin'. . . . Somebody said:
'That's the gamest bastard this side of hell.'

"Yes, Big Stiff, that little black chorus gal
Makes me think of that hot mama
I met at that dance in El Paso. See?
What the hell? I'll be damn . . . Big Stiff.
Sittin' up here sleepin' like a snake on a log,
An' me payin' your way to the show with my good money!
You're a helluva pal . . . you are."

James Killmer

He is going mad . . . this Georgia boy
Who shows you his medals for gallant action in battle
And laughs his hideous laugh.
The Lethean years have passed him by, untouched,
And to every visitor he recites the horrors of no-man's-land,
And in his dreams he lives again those life-in-death eternities.

Like the ebb and flow of tides
The horrors repeat themselves:
Crawling yellow gas,
His face in the rot of a headless corpse,
The shell-crazed Senegalese begging to die,
The Beale Street sweet man
With his intestines in his hands,
The corporal who slept while the rats ate off his face,
His hometown pal
Caught on a live wire
Crying for help in a rainy night,
The hard-boiled sergeant butchered by a laughing madman,
Stench from a thousand putrid bodies,
Hordes of rats with swollen bellies,
Swarms of bloated flies,
Jokes of drudging grave diggers . . .
And above the mud and filth the awful symphony of booming guns.

He is going mad . . . this Georgia boy
Who shows you his medals for gallant action in battle
And laughs his hideous laugh.

Noble Fetchit

Gonna eat an' sleep
An' sing the blues.
Gonna have my women
An' drink my booze,
'Cause a black ain't got
A thing to lose.

Hoed cotton in Alabam
Till my back got as crooked as a snake's.
Picked so many bales of cotton
That my fingers got as raw as beef.
Boss man tells me if I works hard enough . . .
Works a little harder . . .
I might git outa debt.
Looked at his soft white hands an' fine big house
An' tells him I'm shakin' the dust of Alabam
From off my heels.

Worked next in a coal mine in West Virginny.
Worked twelve hours a day an' got the rheumatism.
Et so much sow's belly an' corn pone
That I dreamed the angels
Was eatin' the same 'way up in heaven.
Boss man come down to see us in a big Cadillac an' fur coat
An' tells us the coal mine
Ain't producin' nothin' a-tall.
So I drops my pick an' shovel
An' tells him to take his gawddamn coal mine
An' go straight to hell!

Ridin' the freights all the way to New Yawk,
I thinks an' thinks an' thinks:
Them that rides in big Cadillacs an' wears fur coats
Don't pick no cotton
An' don't work in no coal mines.

Gonna eat an' sleep
An' sing the blues.
Gonna have my women
An' drink my booze,
'Cause a black ain't got
A thing to lose.

Mammy Tyler

Honey, 'tain't no use to act like dat.
Don't cut off de big toe to punish de foot.
I knows how you feel, workin' an' slavin'
When yo' husband ain't got no good in his heart.
I's been through it all maself.
Gawd knows I been tried in de fiery furnace of life!

Yo' own daddy wasn't no Jesus, Honey.
I ain't never told you about dis befo' . . . .
One day I got tired of it all,
An' I packed my things to leave
Yo' daddy an' you chillen.
I hopes Gawd has blotted dat outa de Jedgment Book!

Jest den de spirit of my daid mammy . . .
Yo' grandmammy . . . comes into de room.
I seen her jest as plain as I sees you,
A-settin' in dat chair dat she give me
Befo' she went up in de chariot of de Lawd Gawd.

She says to me jest like I's talkin' to you:
"Chile, if you leaves dem little chillen,
You ain't never gonna see no peace in dis world.
Dey little eyes will follow you wherever you goes.
Dey little voices will call dey mammy day an' night.
Dey little hands will be reachin' out to you all de time.
Don't leave yo' chillen, Chile, don't do dat."

I listened to dat voice of my daid mammy,
An' I obeyed an' it saved me from misery to dis day.
What would you think of me, Honey,
If I'd run off an' left you
When you was a po', little, helpless baby?
What would you think of me now
If I'd made you ashamed of yo' family
In front of yo' little playmates?

I'll tell you, Honey,
A low-down dirty dawg is better dan a woman
Who runs off an' leaves to a friendless world
Her own flesh-an'-blood!

Don't cry like dat, Honey.
I didn't mean to make you cry.
Yo' mammy jest wants to save her chile from misery.
Now straighten up yo' face . . . an' smile.
Dat's it. Now, jest let me put dat suitcase in de closet.
Dat's right! Glory to de Lamb of Gawd!
Set down, Honey. Do you feel better now? Good!

We all has troubles, Honey.
But you cain't git away from trouble
By runnin' away from trouble.
You hasta stand right here, toe to toe,
An' fight it out with Ole Man Trouble!

Prince Banmurji

Prince Banmurji, heir of Zulu kings,
Adopted son of Harvard and Oxford,
Famous authority on African customs and dialects and music,
Strolled up Seventh Avenue on New Year's Eve,
Passing Negroes of every ethnic feature and hue.
This was what the melting pot had done
To the sons and daughters of his fatherland!

The prince was a spiritual hybrid,
An amalgam of the first generation
In an alien culture.
The Aframerican was at home,
Having lost the vestiges of African thought patterns.

Western concepts and customs
Had split the prince's personality.
If in Harlem,
He yearned for the simplicity of Africa;
If in his native land,
For the delights of Paris and London and New York.
He knew the virtues and vices
Of both barbarism and civilization.
Thus Prince Banmurji had lived a fuller life
Than either the savage or the sophisticate.
Life is the sum of a man's experiences.

"Mixed races are more interesting," he mused,
As he bumped into an ancient black woman
Untouched by the rape of the conqueror.

The prince shifted his ivory cane,
With the dexterity of a cavalier,
And raised his vivid black derby.

"Madam, I beg your pardon,"
Came the precise Oxford accents.
The ancient woman grumbled:
"You oughta watch whar you's gwine."
Prince Banmurji luxuriated:
"I was thinking, Madam, thinking."

Etchings

Jake Bunner

Jake Bunner has gone home to his poor old mother
In Shreveport, Louisiana.
He has gone to work for old Judge Shearing
Near Centenary College.
He has joined the Church of God on Looney Street.
He has married little Elissa Long,
The mother of his six-year-old son.

Down on Texas Avenue at the bus station,
Jake cried on Aunt Dinah's billowy bosom
And told her how her prayers
Had followed him to wicked Harlem
And how God . . . Glory to his name! . . .
Had compelled him to return
To his Christian mother.

In front of startled whites and blacks,
Aunt Dinah smothered him in her magnanimous arms
And her tearful joy voiced itself in song:
>   *Done found my lost sheep,*
>   *Done found my lost sheep,*
>   *Done found my lost sheep.*

But Jake did not tell Aunt Dinah
How his still had exploded in his flat on New Year's Eve
And caused a terrible conflagration
Destroying half of a city block.
Jake did not tell Aunt Dinah
That the police of New York City had cast a dragnet for him.

Pearl Tripplett

Come on, Daddy, come on,
What makes you so slow?
Come on, Daddy, come on,
What makes you so slow?
If you's a homeless daddy,
Yo' babe knows whar to go.

Pearl makes her nocturnal trips
Along One Hundred and Fifteenth Street.
She is like a tramp of the tropics,
Stopping at any disreputable port
To pick up cargo.

When de gold is in de mud,
It ain't never gonna shine.
When de soil ain't black an' rich,
'Tain't no crop a-lookin' fine.
Lawdy . . . Lawdy . . . Lawdy!

If Pearl's mother
Had not left her little daughter
Under the too-loving care
Of old Uncle Billy,
While she worked twelve hours a day
In the white folks's kitchen . . .
Perhaps . . .
Pearl would not be picking up cargo
In the nocturnal shadows
Along One Hundred and Fifteenth Street.

The Biggest Fool in Harlem

Peter Osgood is the biggest fool in Harlem.
As his only friend, I tell him so . . .
And he throws back his head and belly laughs.

Everybody is afraid of him,
Because you never can tell what he'll say or do.
Discovering skeletons in high places
And exhibiting them to the dark masses,
He triumphs to the rafters of Liberty Hall:
"The truth shall make you free!"

When he was Grand Secretary
Of the Sons and Daughters of Ethiopia,
Like a black Samson Agonistes,
He toppled the financial pillars of the organization
In his annual report to the Grand Conclave.

Mr. Knapp Sackville,
Grand Chancellor and Most Exalted Polemarch,
Almost collapsed in the Exalted Chair;
And the eyes of Grand Treasurer Gladstone Milkum
Almost popped from his bullet head.

Peter Osgood was not re-elected:
Mr. Knapp Sackville in his annual address
Accused the Grand Secretary, incumbent,
Of accepting blood money from Moscow
And failing to cooperate
With the administration.

When the Mt. Pisgah Baptists
Bought that second-hand church from the white folk,
Peter Osgood was chairman of the Board of Deacons.
His fiscal report to the membership
Sent the Reverend Truce Steele untimely
To his God.

Not another preacher has put Osgood on a Board of Deacons.
Not another grand chancellor has made him a secretary.

You see . . .
When everything is going smoothly
Among the Big Niggers on Sugar Hill,
Peter Osgood stirs up trouble.
He's the biggest fool in Harlem.

He goes about prying into things and saying:
"The truth shall make you free!"

As if somebody wanted to be free.

Faith Hanley

Good Hope Baptist Church pitied Faith
When she married Zion Hanley, the drunkard.
The night Little Jennie was born
Zion came staggering in,
To the disgust of Sister Cripens.

Faith consulted the Reverend Isaac Evans,
And in the preacher's small study
Both prayed for the erring husband.
During the fall revival
Zion came to the Mourners' Bench and repented.

After that, things went from bad to worse,
Like a patched tire,
And twice Zion sobered up in jail
With a heavy fine.

On Christmas Eve, Zion returned from celebrating
With his liquor-loving cronies,
And fell across the bed.

Faith had taken a lesson from Sister Cripens;
So she stripped her insensible husband
And roped him securely.

Then she took the belt from his work clothes . . .
The broad, thick belt that made Zion look manly . . .
And beat him until his yellow buttocks
Became black and blue.

Zion begged and begged for mercy,
And promised never . . . never . . .
To taste another drink of liquor;
But Faith continued to belabor him and lecture him
Until she was exhausted.

Zion was unable to sit down for a week.
He had to sleep upon his belly.
He sulked.
He swore
He was going to get even with Faith,
But a glimpse
Of the little devil in her eye
Weakened his resolution.

Good Hope Baptist Church
Marvels at the change in Zion Hanley.
Aunt Tommiezene sighs:
"Love will find a way."
The Reverend Isaac Evans huzzahs:
"The prayers of the righteous availeth much."

Sister Cripens and Faith Hanley
Shake hands on Sunday
And exchange knowing glances,
While inquiring after each other's health.

Carrie Green

Carrie drags her aching feet up the dirty stairs . . .

Nobody knows de trouble I seen,
Nobody knows but Jesus.

Weariness swells in her body,
Weariness too big for her body
And the four dingy walls of Mr. Maranto's café.

Away down in Vicksburg,
White-haired Miss Smithfield . . .

Ole Massa Grant he took Vicksburg
To set de darkies free . . .

Dear Miss Smithfield told Carrie
That the blacks were poor
Because God was punishing them for their laziness;
But that if Carrie would be thrifty,
Like white folk,
She could lay aside enough money for her old age.

Good Miss Smithfield is now in heaven . . .

Glory to de Lamb of Gawd! . . .

For Carrie heard the dear lady say,
On her deathbed,
That God was calling His servant home.

During the hard, hard years
Carrie worked faithfully and saved what she could;
But her pitiable sum was lost
In the collapse of the Security National Bank.

Nevertheless,
Faith can move mountains . . .
So Carrie goes to Mr. Maranto's café at 6 A.M.
And works over the red-hot stove till 6 P.M.
And climbs the dirty stairs,
Tired in body and spirit,
Just as she used to be
When good Miss Smithfield,
Now in heaven,
Worked her fourteen hours a day
And gave her two dollars a week
And cast-off clothes
And good advice.

Horace Allyn

When Horace encountered painful realities,
He hid himself
In the shell of his egoism.

He liked pretty things
In art and music and everyday life.
Syrupy lyrics and poetical preachments
Stirred him profoundly.

The electric constellations along Seventh Avenue
Interested him more
Than the flowing dusky multitude
With its side-street tributaries.

Horace scorned the poor and ignorant of his race,
Ridiculing them . . . abusing them;
He condemned white Southerners for their prejudices
And Communists for their radicalism.

Horace censured O'Neill for *The Emperor Jones*,
Despised Paul Robeson for playing the nigger crapshooter,
Castigated Richard B. Harrison for his role of De Lawd,
Denounced Langston Hughes with his blackamoor ballads,
And considered hell too good for Cab Calloway
With his Minnie the Moocher and hi-de-ho mannerisms.

Horace often shocked his prudish wife by saying:
"Thelma, when I get to heaven,
I shall ask God,
As soon as I see Him,
Why in the hell he made me a nigger."

Dr. Cram Mifflin

Dr. Mifflin's knowledge of women had come from books;
So his colleagues snickered when he came to Harlem
To make a study of the Negro servant girl
For a foundation directed by paternalistic whites.

The Professor of Sociology at Hoare University,
Which granted one dubious degree,
Diademed the college catalogue
With his A.B., A.M., Ph.D., and Litt.D.

He walked the graveled paths
With his pigmy hands clasped behind him,
His eyes fixed on the invisible.
You insulted him if you did not call him "Doctor"
To distinguish him from the other professors.

He craved popularity with the students,
Although pillorying them for their ignorance.
They nicknamed him "Bantam."

In faculty meetings he upset President Dunn and Dean Greene
By referring everlastingly to the academic methods
Of Yale and Columbia and Cambridge.
He finished every argument as if he were saying:
"Thus saith the Lord God!"

He has written President Dunn and Dean Greene
That his study of the Negro servant girl in Harlem
Requires a longer leave of absence.
A physician is treating Dr. Mifflin
For the data he received one night from a buxom laundress.

Uncle Rufus

The Harlem Advocate fell between his legs.
The story was incredible!
Taking off his glasses,
Uncle Rufus rubbed the lenses and thought . . . thought.

Yes, his son had always been a prodigal son,
Drinking home brew and chasing sin-loving women
And staying away from church at revival times.

Then he had gone to Selma, Alabama,
With that Blackwood woman
Who had lived with a dozen different sweet men.

The Harlem Advocate said
Eddie had cut up the Blackwood woman in a dance hall;
And, when the jury had found him guilty,
He'd struck the prosecuting attorney on the jaw;
And it had taken the jurors and a deputy sheriff
To pin him to the floor and handcuff him.

Uncle Rufus bowed his head and groaned.
He remembered now that people used to say
Eddie was a little off . . . a little off.

"De boy musta been crazy," Uncle Rufus mused aloud.
"Yes, he musta been crazy . . .
Him hittin' a white lawyah
In a white man's courthouse,
Befo' a white jedge an' a white jury
Down in Alabama."

Okay Katie

Dat big red moon in Harlem
Dat makes de heavens bright as day
Ain't half so fine to look at
Since Okay Katie went away.

She was born in an office building
Where her mother scrubbed floors at night;
And in the arms of transient lovers
She made her living at night;
And the dark ruin of her was carried
From a small house of God
To be buried at night.

Alas,
The bodies and spirits
Of no more Harlem lovers
Will find sweet relief
In the bedroom of Okay Katie.

Her toil-broken mother is dumb with grief;
Her high-toned sister is secretly glad
That the insurance policy is good;
And her soft-living man wonders
If he will ever find another woman
As wise in the ways of making love . . .
As easy on her sweet man's hootchiepap-chasing . . .
And as free with her pocketbook
As Okay Katie was in her good-timing days.

Mrs. Ernest Quirk

The very night I married Dr. Quirk
He came into the living room drunk and raped me.

Mine is an old Virginian family
With a rich heritage of culture.
My maternal grandfather was a Negro senator
During the Reconstruction Period,
And my paternal grandmother
The daughter of a Southern governor
Who educated her in Paris.
She was much admired for her beauty
By Alexander Dumas, pere.

Dr. Quirk has no cultural background
And no appreciation of such.
His father was an illiterate street cleaner
And his mother a washerwoman.

I used to remind Dr. Quirk
That blood will tell.
He would sneer:
"You're right, my dear.
In everybody there is the blood
Of genius and idiot, saint and blackguard."

Dr. Quirk is a man of filthy habits:
He bathes only on Saturday nights,
Dips snuff,
Puts his feet against the walls,
Slaps female patients on their posteriors,
And tells vulgar stories even among the elite.

On Saturday nights he gives chitterling suppers.
Greasy politicians, ungodly preachers,
Cabaret entertainers, policy bankers,
And other Harlem riffraff
Take possession of the apartment
And play poker and shoot craps till dawn.
Sometimes they become so rowdy
The neighbors send for the police.
The officers clap Dr. Quirk on the back,
Take a good drink, and leave smoking his cigars.

I bore his vulgarities as long as possible
For the sake of my family.
The children and I are going to mother's.
I shall divorce Dr. Quirk immediately.

74

Grandma Grady

"Wife of Prominent Physician to Sue for Divorce!
Society Arbiter Leaves for Richmond with Children!"

Now, Lawd, here it is . . .
Spread all over the front page
Of *The Harlem Advocate*.

Kin you beat that!
I been cleanin' up Dr. Quirk's office
Fer nigh unto fifteen years,
An' I ain't seen a kinder-hearted man
In all my borned days.

I ain't never liked that woman
The first time I laid eyes on her.
She useta pass me jest like I was a piece of dirt . . .
Haid up in the air like a giraffe.

Dr. Quirk says she was crazy
With them 'lusions of persecution.
If she couldn't have her way,
She'd scream at the top of her voice,
Accuse 'im of chasin' pretty whores,
Throw dishes an' flowerpots at 'im,
An' break into his office
When he was waitin' on women patients.
I've seen 'im come to work many a time
With his face all scratched up.

Everybody in Harlem likes Dr. Quirk,
High an' low, rich an' poor.
He never asks a patient to pay his bills.
He'll call on a bum jest as quick
As one of the Big Niggers on Sugar Hill.
He contributes to four or five churches,
An' to widows an' orphans.
He ain't never passed a beggar
Without givin' 'im somethin'.

Yes, Dr. Quirk is a good man . . .
Too good fer that hussy,
Even if her family tree is tall
As the Empire State Buildin'.

Richmond Hoover

For thirty years The Hoover Meat Company
Had catered to a proud middle class
Of white customers,
And Richmond Hoover boasted
That he carried only choice cuts of meat.

Maiden ladies and the wives of small businessmen,
Who were more interested
In the quality of the commodity than in its price,
Looked upon Richmond Hoover as an equal.

Then came the dusky waves of the World War migration,
And the little proprietor saw with great trepidation
His erstwhile white customers washed to other shores.
Richmond Hoover called the dark influx the black plague.

But he refused to stock his shop with cheaper meats,
And he failed to lower his prices.
He sat in his spacious chair,
White-aproned, dignified, scornful,
While the Negroes entered the Jew's market on the corner.

The old shopkeeper announced one evening:
"I shall not alter the policy and service
Of The Hoover Meat Company
For filthy lucre and the patronage of niggers."

Unobserved, his invalid wife flinched . . .
And nodded her small head in affirmation.

Old Man Salem

Old Man Salem did not know
That he was a descendant of the black Peter Salem
Who killed Major Pitcairn at Bunker Hill.

Old Man Salem got up early
Before Eighth Avenue became feverish
With the hurrying feet of tight-faced workers.
Old Man Salem made his rounds
Before other early birds
Filched the choice scraps
From the neighborhood garbage cans.

Old Man Salem was abroad
Before his sharp-tongued landlady,
Who saw even crooked things crooked,
Worked her protesting bulk out of bed
And poked her fantastic plaits into the hallway
To catch some luckless roomer
Slipping a companion from her respectable house.

Sometimes Old Man Salem chanced upon
A pair of rickety shoes or a dilapidated coat;
Then his little eyes burned brightly
Like those of a Pasteur
In a moment of discovery.

Brothah, if they don't know nothing 'bout you,
They cain't say nothing 'bout you,
Praise the Lawd!

Dr. Harvey Whyte

Black Boy, why you cryin'
In de lonesome night?
De Lawd when He's paintin'
Didn't paint me white.
Dat's de reason Black Boy's
Cryin' in de night!

It's a long, hard road
From the Flint Plantation
At Waycross, Georgia,
To the position of chief surgeon
In a Harlem hospital.

It's a long, hard road
For a beggarly black boy.

And that pitiless road
Had sapped the humor
From the heart
Of. Dr. Harvey Whyte
And drained the sentiment
From his soul.

Victor Garibaldi

It was a glorious May morning
Tingling with the joy of life.

Victor's hand organ
Was grinding out a merry tune
While Little Caesar the monkey,
Dudish in his frock coat and shining high hat,
Strutted up and down the sidewalk.

A dusky woman stood at the open window
Of a flat on the fourth floor,
Dabbing at her eyes
With a damp linen handkerchief.

Victor, smiling broadly,
Extended his gay-colored straw hat.
The dusky face was a sorrowful mask
As the brown hand
Traced an arc between the lace curtains.

Surprised and curious,
Victor Garibaldi,
The descendant of the red-shirted liberator of Italy,
Gazed a long, long time
At the vacant, open window
Through which the dusky woman
Had tossed her new wedding ring.

It was a glorious May morning
Tingling with the joy of life.

Lena Lovelace

> When ma baby shouts in church
>   I likes to be about.
> When ma baby shouts in church
>   I likes to be about.
> I knows she'll be like honey
>   When de lights go out.

James and Lena sat side by side
One Sunday night
In the Good Hope Baptist Church,
While the Reverend Isaac Evans preached his famous sermon,
Dry Bones in the Valley.
Sweeping grandly to his climax, he cried:
"Can these dry bones live?"

"Yes!" screamed Lena, leaping to her feet.
A stout dark sister ducked her fat head
When Lena, flinging her arms wide,
Began shouting up and down the aisle,
Her breath coming in gasps and her eyes staring fixedly.
The church swelled with lusty amens
And the preacher paused, grinning his approbation.

As Lena made her way to the rostrum,
James's appreciative eyes pursued the yellow dress
Drawn tightly about her joggling hips.
James liked to see his wife shout in church at night . . .
It was those nights that she made love the best.

Sergeant Tiffin

You can't tell what's in a man
Till it has a chance to come out.

> *Ole men spends dey money*
> *On gay young gals, y'know.*
> *Old men spends dey money*
> *On gay young gals, y'know.*
> *Young bucks don't do nothin'*
> *But hoe de ole men's row.*

Sergeant Tiffin, my granduncle, was ninety-five
When he married Ida, the strappin' pretty widow
Who sent Daddy Oldfield to an early grave
With too much lovin'.

Folks waited for the report
Of old Sergeant Tiffin's death . . .
Waited in vain.

A year later
Ida gave birth to a healthy, ten-pound son!
Dr. Harvey Whyte, pullin' his goatee,
Called in some big-shot doctors.
They put their heads together.
They shook their heads and winked and grinned.

Mother Vibbard, who's seen twenty-five presidents come and go,
Said to Sister Cripens one night after prayer meetin':
"I ain't heard of a thing like dis in all ma borned days!
Sistah Cripens, some young buck is helpin' ole Tiffin
To hoe his potato patch. It's a shame befo' Gawd!"

> *A man's loss*
> *Is a woman's gain.*
> *A man's joy*
> *Is a woman's pain.*

Sergeant Tiffin was like a young stud comin' of age.
Ida? Ida was like a sun gone down on a wintry day.
She hated the child more and more . . . the more she saw it.

Sister Cripens, the biggest gossip in Harlem,
Dropped in on Ida and sympathized with her deeply.
Sister Cripens rocked the baby to sleep
And looked at it a long time . . . a long time.

The next day she said to Mother Vibbard:
"De chile is de spittin' image of ole Sergeant Tiffin!"

You can't tell what's in a man
Till it has a chance to come out.

Augustus Lence

When a man is down
He's all alone.
When a man is down
He's all alone,
Like a homeless dawg
Without a bone.

Augustus sat on the stoop in the November night.
Oblong patterns of yellow radiance
Shaped themselves
Along the naked ugliness of tenements.

A block away,
A homing elevated train
Stabbed the Harlem night
With blades of light and sound.

When you's got de blues
'Tain't no use to pray.
When you's got de blues
'Tain't no use to pray.
Takes a brown-skin gal
To chase de blues away.

Now and then
A solitary pedestrian passed,
Like a phantom
Crossing a shadowy waste
Of flat water.

The moon,
A disc of burnished brass,
Floated beyond a ruin of dark ashen cloud.
The stars
Were vivid fireflies
Glowing in an azure desolation.

If I had some arms
A good mile long,
Some arms, Lawd, Lawd,
A good mile long,
I'd reach out ma hands
Whar ma baby's gone!

Augustus sat on the stoop in the November night.
The chill in his heart was like
The chill in the street,
And his mind harbored a ruin of desolate dreams.

But there was no moon and there were no stars
To brighten the sky of his destiny.

Zip Lightner

Big Boss settin' in de shade
Drinkin' whiskey-lemonade.
Tenant farmers work like hell
Raisin' cotton fer to sell!

Yes, Black Boy, de Jedgment Day is comin' . . .
An' it won't be no thousand years a-gittin' here.
I finds dat out in White River County, Arkansas.
An' I don't mean maybe!

I useta say neither Gawd nor de devil
Could git de poor whites an' blacks together.
Bless my soul . . . de Union was organized
Right dere in my own cabin.

Big Boss sends his kids to school,
Lookin' nice an' lookin' cool.
Tenants' kids grow up like weeds,
Ain't got nothin' dat dey needs.

Planter bosses seen de sharecroppers mean business.
At de meetin's in de Marked Tree Baptist Church,
Even de women an' chillen come . . .
Jest like dey was enterin' de Promised Land.
You shoulda heard de speeches an' de singin'!
Some of de folks cried fer joy.

De ridin' bosses burned down de church.
Uncle Amos was lynched on Dainger Point.
Cabins was riddled wid bullets.
Minnie Ross was shot wid a baby in her arms.

When dey pays off in de fall,
Lawd, de Big Boss takes it all.
Tenants stand it fer a spell;
Den de Union raises hell!

De Union brung me to New Yawk
To make speeches in Liberty Hall.
De People wants to know what we sharecroppers
Is doin' an' thinkin' down in Arkansas.
De People is with us.

De People suffers a long time, Black Boy.
De People gits hongry an' hongry. Den de People wakes up.
De People wants to know
Who in de hell give de Big Bosses de right
To put dey damn foot on de People's neck!
Den de People stands up,
Like Gawd intended from de beginnin' of time,
An' de People asks de Big Bosses:

"By Gawd, ain't dis a government of de People,
By de People, an' fer de People?"

Black Boy, dat's what brings de Jedgment Day . . .
An' it won't be no thousand years a-gittin' here.
I finds dat out in White River County, Arkansas.
An' I don't mean maybe!

Old Pettigrew

Along Lenox Avenue folk said
Old Pettigrew had sold himself to the devil.

Beneath the confusion of a filthy sheet
His wasted body was clammy
With the cold damp of a fever.
The hooch bought from the little Sicilian
Had left his throat seared and raw.

As he lay dying,
Praying John attempted to persuade him
To make his peace with God.

Old Pettigrew cursed both God and the preacher
While death rattled its portent
In his throat.

That wintry afternoon
Pedestrians on Lenox Avenue
Gazed in bewilderment
At a hatless preacher in an ancient Prince Albert coat
Dashing up from a dingy basement room,
Pursued by wraiths of insane laughter.

Praying John has frightened
Many a sinner into the Kingdom
By telling how he was on his knees
Praying for the soul of Old Pettigrew
When the devil laughed under the deathbed.

Uncle Walt

When you has drunk de sweets of life,
Why stay down here in pain an' strife?

Gawd knows dat workin' on a elevator day after day
Is a no-man's job . . . a no-man's job.
But I useta work in one of de finest stables
In ma ole Kentucky home,
Befo' ma kidney went bad an' ma feets no good.

Lawdy, Lawdy,
Puttin' a he-man like me on a job like dis
Is de same as tyin' a racehoss in his stall
When de blood in him is a-cryin' fer de racetrack,
Wid de crowds an' de band an' de cheerin'.

I's a outside man . . . dat's all . . .
An' Gawd knows I don't like no inside, no-man's job.
Howsomever . . . says I to maself . . .
What kin I do wid a bad kidney an' no-good feets?

I don't like de carryin' on around here,
Sich as de other night
When dat woman run screamin' down de hall:
"Uncle Walt, start de elevator quick as hell!"

When Gawd made woman He done His best,
But Gawd an' man ain't had no rest.

Jest as she gits on, a big man rushes up
An' snatches de woman off by de haid an' says:
"You's stayin' wid me tonight, you bitch!"

Remember dat dis Lonesome Road's
Got many a rut an' bend.
What's gonna happen, no one knows
Until you reach de end.

Dar was a slick-lookin' Eyetalian
Dat useta ride de elevator.
He always tipped me two bits a day,
But I'd never heard him say nothin' a-tall.
Jest stood dar in de cage chewin' his gum.

Last week I took 'im up to de tenth floor.
You kin see how skeered I was
When he run back into de elevator, cryin':
"Uncle Walt! Uncle Walt!"

'Bout dat time another Eyetalian popped up
An' pumped 'im full of holes wid an automatic.
"You gawddamn rat!" he said.

Gawd knows I ain't got no love fer dis job . . .
None a-tall.
Howsomever . . . says I to maself . . .
What kin I do wid a bad kidney an' no-good feets?

Juarez Mary

Gold Tooth Looney used to sing in his sober periods:

> *Easy come an' easy go . . .*
> *You don't know an' I don't know*
> *When a jinx will stop the show.*

Juarez Mary is lying on a cold slab
In a Harlem morgue . . .
Juarez Mary, who knew every dope hawk and sweet man
On Upper Lenox Avenue.

Ten years ago she left a cheap casino
Below the Rio Grande,
And came by a devious route to Nigger Heaven,
With Gold Tooth Looney,
The snare drummer who promised her an easy life.

Gold Tooth Looney showed Juarez Mary the bright lights.
She liked the hot women and good-timing prizefighters,
The high-stepping entertainers and spendthrift actors.

Gold Tooth Looney was killed one night
In a crap game on Strivers' Row;
And Juarez Mary, rudderless,
Drifted into the rotten seas of Harlem's underworld.

A cop found Juarez Mary at dawn
With twenty-nine cents and some cocaine
In her shabby pocketbook.
A cop found Juarez Mary in a deserted entranceway
With her throat slit from ear to ear.

Isidor Lawson

He had worked as a busboy and waiter
From Palm Beach to Atlantic City . . .
From Galveston to St. Paul.

Little did the guests imagine
That the silent young man who served them
Was studying their faces and habits and conversations
And dreaming of a higher level of living.

At a hotel on the Gold Coast of Chicago
Isidor Lawson waited on old Mr. Curtis Rivers.
After every meal the grim financier
Left a penny under his plate.
Discovering six months later Isidor had saved the pennies,
The eccentric gave him five dollars for each of them. . . .

Mr. Lawson and his highbrow wife worship
At the Abyssinia Baptist Church,
The largest Christian membership in the world.

If Mr. Lawson finds an employee or a guest
Violating any of the regulations in the Hotel Harlem,
He deals in a summary manner.

> Through swingin' doors of hotel lobbies
>   De people come an' go.
> What happens, Black Boy, in de rooms
>   Gawd an' de bellhops know!

Mr. Lawson does not hear his employees belly laugh
Whenever they see the respectability of the Hotel Harlem
Advertised in *The Harlem Advocate*.

Chef Sam Logan

His feet were flat as his pancakes.
Behind his back
The bellhops and cooks and waiters and chambermaids
Called Chef Sam Logan "Foots."
He had worked with Isidor Lawson
In a Little Rock hotel,
And his boss had paid his railroad fare North.

"Foots" had married Lola Mae,
Lawson's baby sister,
And the hotel gossips said she led him a dog's life.
She didn't have red hair for nothing!

Through a keyhole, a chambermaid saw her
In bed, naked, with the late Diamond Canady.

> *She's a red-hot mama*
> *With a million-dollar swing.*
> *It makes my love come down*
> *To see her shake dat thing.*

The soft-voiced captain of bellhops
Was the joy of the hostesses at the Savoy,
Harlem's premier ballroom.
Lola Mae entertained him in an upstairs chamber
While "Foots" was on the job.

If Chef Sam Logan suspected anything,
Not a soul could tell . . .
For he shuffled about in the kitchen as usual,
Grinning and cracking jokes.

Hamuel Gutterman

>*Happy days is here again—*
No change in the Mongolian cast of his countenance.

Sometimes, when the Hotel Harlem was asleep,
He talked to the night porter or a bellhop
About Karl Marx and Friederich Engels and George Hegel.

Hamuel Gutterman said
That if all the bourgeois Negro leaders
Were piled in a pyramid as high as Cheops
They wouldn't be worth the feces of an ass!
>*Dat sho' is one big lie.*
>*Ain't et a pork chop in so long*
>*My belly wants to cry!*

His egg-shaped head was set on a squat body
That ballooned in the belt
And slanted into spindle legs.

His peon-father was in a chain gang at Yazoo City
For beating up a white planter
In an argument over a bale of cotton.

Whatever emotion stirred in Hamuel Gutterman,
There was no change in the droning bass of his voice.

Ferenc Glaspell

His oily face ridged with a moony grin,
Ferenc, the night porter, was obsequious
In the presence of his superiors;
But among his fellow workers
His ugliness bristled with arrogance.

Gutterman taught him to operate
The telephone switchboard.
While the disciple of Karl Marx slept like those of Jesus,
Ferenc promoted his own impious deals.
The bellhops hated him,
But they did not hate the extra tips.

>   *A man hasta live.*
>   *If you ask me why,*
>   *A man hasta live*
> *'Cause he's skeered to die.*

Under the guise of efficiency,
Ferenc gained the confidence of Mr. Lawson;
And the cynical Gutterman saw in him
A proletarian flunky of the boss system.

One evening Mr. Lawson caught the night porter
Slipping Lola Mae up the fire escape
To the room of Gloomy Dean.

Five minutes later, Mr. Lawson discharged Ferenc.
As the ex-porter walked from the lobby into 135th Street,
Chef Sam Logan sprang from behind a parked car
And knocked him down . . . breaking his neck.

Laura Yost

In Major Dunne's ricefields
Down in the Red River Valley,
Rheumatism had fastened itself
On Laura's widowed mother,
Twisting her hands and legs.

When Laura went to work at the Hotel Harlem,
The manager told her to watch as well as pray:
It was not his policy to employ
Young and good-looking women as chambermaids.
For five or six months
Laura followed his advice.

Then she succumbed to the lure
Of gaudy dresses and flashy jewels and garish toilet articles,
Which garrulous traveling salesmen displayed before her.

It took her meager wages
To take care of her grumbling mother.
And, oh, how her heart ached with envy
When she saw the finery of the other girls
In Galilee Baptist Church!

Mr. Lawson discovered Laura stretched out
Under the salesman for the Race Pride Fashion Company.
Laura is now
A streetwalker and blasphemous mother
Who knows not the father of her child.

Uriah Houze

Uriah was drafted into the army;
And for the first time he left
The crisscross ridges of Kentucky
Where he had worked
With Old Haily, the moonshiner
Who had adopted him as an infant.

Uriah knew nothing about his parentage.
Old Haily was coming home half-drunk one night.
As he passed an abandoned tourist camp
On the outskirts of Clay City
He heard a baby crying.
That was how he came to find little Uriah
Lying on a dirty quilt in a washtub.

When Uriah returned from France,
He saw the bright lights of Harlem
And hated to go back
To the crisscross ridges of Kentucky.
But he loved the old white moonshiner.

It was the darkest moment in Uriah's life
When a crossroads storekeeper in the hill country
Told him Old Haily had been killed
By a revenue officer.
Uriah was glad Old Haily had got his man!

Uriah learned many things from the old moonshiner,
And Uriah makes the best bootleg whiskey on Lenox Avenue.
He hates the Law
Worse than carbolic acid,
And above the mantlepiece in his flat
Hangs Old Haily's Winchester.
It has thirteen notches.

Sidney Sippel

Life kin take a Lindy Hop, Black Boy, an' mess you up.
Dat's what skeers de hell outa me!
Here we is . . . you an' me . . .
Settin' in dis spooky flat on 116th Street
Wid de back-to-dust body of Sidney Sippel.

Me an'him was in France together.
Oncet we went over de top side by side,
An' he come back wid three bullet holes in his clothes
An' not a scratch on his skin.
Another time his heel was shot clear off his shoe,
But his foot wasn't even singed.

Now, Black Boy, if he hadn't stopped at dat fillin' station
At Tombstone, Arizona, dat evenin'
He'd be here among de livin' . . .
Jest like you an' me.
Life is a helluva thing, Black Boy, wid its Lindy Hops.

Sippel was a Pullman porter in Los Angeles.
While he was out on his runs,
His lonesome wife, Stella,
Starts cabaretin' wid another woman.
Dat woman's got a voice . . . Stella has . . .
Like nobody else in Gawd's creation.
It's a graveyard voice . . .
If you know what I mean . . .
Wid de loneliness of de world in it.

One night in a honky-tonk on Central Avenue
When the orchestra is playin' de "St. Louis Blues,"
Stella gits up half-drunk an' starts singin'.
De folks tear up de cabaret.
One homesick bastard cries an' pukes.
A Cracker from Atlanta gives her a hundred dollars.

After dat Stella gits crazy to go on de stage.
While Sippel is in Seattle, she disappears . . . evaporates.

Fer five years Sippel advertises fer her.
Den he quits de service, buys a second-hand Chevrolet,
An' swears he's gonna find her or die tryin'.

97

Two weeks ago he stops at a fillin' station
At Tombstone, Arizona, to git a flat fixed.
He hears a woman's graveyard voice singin' over de radio
De "St. Louis Blues" in a Harlem night club
Wid Snakehips Flippen's orchestra.

Sippel comes here an' finds Stella.
She is married to a cornet player.
She tells her husband, indignantlike,
She knows nothin' about Sidney Sippel.
She says: "Honey, I ain't seen dis nigger befo'."

Sidney Sippel comes to de flat an' drinks carbolic acid.
Life is a helluva thing, Black Boy, wid its Lindy Hops.

Mrs. Gertrude Beamish

"What will the white folks think?"
Obsessed Mrs. Gertrude Beamish.

The good lady urged her race
To make a favorable impression on white people . . .
The best white people . . .
Since the dark bourgeoisie have nothing but contempt
For the toiling Caucasian masses.

If Negroes dress well and deport themselves
Like ladies and gentlemen in public,
No longer will they be considered
Lazy and ill smelling, sensual and ignorant.

Negroes shouldn't eat chicken and watermelon
In the presence of white people.
Negro women ought to quit dressing
In red and green and yellow.
Negro men should stop wearing Jewish suits
With outlandish stripes.

Several Harlem churches joined the crusade
After the good lady had contributed to the pastor's upkeep.

One evening Mr. Beamish suggested timidly
That a wife's place is in the home,
And Mrs. Beamish let out a long-kept secret:
"You're an uncouth nigger who makes me want to puke
Every time you touch me with your filthy little hands."

Vergil Ragsdale

I's on dat Lonesome Road
An' my heart's like lead.
On dat Lonesome Road, Lawd,
With a heart like lead.
Don't want no mourners
When I's laid out dead!

Vergil knew he had only a few years to live.
It had been his overweening purpose
To save enough money
As dishwasher at Mr. Maranto's café
To give him leisure for the epic of his people . . .
The epic that haunted him day and night.

But standing twelve hours on a damp floor
And bending his frail body over steaming sinks
And walking long distances in the chill night
Had left him tuberculous.

It's hell fer death to come fer you
When you is got a job to do.

He must not die before completing *An African Tragedy*!
For that purpose had he come into the world.
Often he forgot to eat. Sometimes, to sleep.
He worked in an ill-lighted rear room,
Fired by the hectic afflatus that had inspired
Keats and Watteau, Mozart and Chopin.

His vitality ebbing rapidly,
He stimulated himself with gin and cocaine
Bought from Jazz Boker.

The iambic pentameters trooped across the yellow pages
Like colorful soldiers on parade.
But he must not stop to admire them.
He was in a race with death. . . .

Big Sadie, the landlady,
Failing to see Vergil for two days,
Ordered her husband to investigate.

100

He broke into the room and found the poet's body
Lying by the rickety table where it had fallen.

Sniffing disdainfully,
Big Sadie raised the window.
Then she collected the yellow sheets
Containing *An African Tragedy*
And dropped them into the waste basket.

Turning to her husband, she said:
"Put this trash in the furnace."

Jobyna Dear

Lawd, take dat woman by de han'.
She's lost her man, her lovin' man.

Whenever Jobyna entered Mother Zion . . .
Sat in the Lafayette Theatre . . .
Went on a boat excursion up the Hudson . . .
Danced in the Renaissance Casino—
Places where she and Vergil had gone together—
The memory of the tragic poet
Made her dark with yearning and grief.

He had died while she was in Baltimore
Visiting her brother who'd been crippled in a creamery.
She hastened to Big Sadie's
To get the precious manuscript.

"Honey, I saved all his clothes an' letters an' books,"
Big Sadie informed her proudly.
"Don't cry, Chile. I know jest how you feel.
Mr. Vergil was a fine young man.
A little queer, of course . . . scribblin' day an' night.
Howsomever, he didn't chase women like most men.
Men's got dawg in 'em, Honey. S'pose you know that."

I got de blues dere's no denyin'
When I keeps on cryin' an' cryin'
Like my heart is gonna break.

Going to places they'd visited together
Sweetened Jobyna's melancholy.

Several months passed
And Playboy Jeeter came into her life . . .
Playboy Jeeter, full of the ecstasy of living.
His undesigned coming
Was like a flashlight
Scattering the imps of darkness.

On their wedding night,
As she lay in his arms,
A pang of yearning and grief
Cut her to the quick.

She began to cry,
And Playboy Jeeter,
The man about Harlem,
Smiled sagely to himself,
As he tried to comfort her
With the blandishments of the worldly-wise.
Life had taught him many things about virgins.

But how was he to know
That his wife was crying . . .
Because she had not given herself to another?

Jack D'Orsay

The nightlife of Harlem caught Jack D'Orsay
In its jazz rhythms
Like a piece of jetsam in a maelstrom.

The money he brought to the dark city
Disappeared like a rabbit
In a magician's act.

He tramped through the uncompanionable streets
Looking for work;
But trying to find a job in New York City
Was like searching for snowflakes
In the Sahara.

> *Ain't got nothing to do, Baby.*
> *Lawd, Lawd, nothing to do,*
> *But dream sweet dreams of you.*

The police of Atlanta wanted Jack D'Orsay
For the murder of a stool pigeon.
He thought of that whenever the yearning came
To see his invalid father.

"I's going down home," said Jack D'Orsay,
"When Harlem becomes the capital of Georgy."

He sat drooped on a corner of his dirty cot,
Thrumming the banjo of his invalid father
And singing in a funereal monotone:

> *Ain't got nothing to do, Baby.*
> *Lawd, Lawd, nothing to do,*
> *But dream sweet dreams of you.*

Mrs. Josephine Wise

If Johnny raided the box in the pantry
And his mother discovered him with some of the cookies,
The dear lady would sigh: "Stealing . . . just like a nigger!"

If Johnny got into a fight on his way from school
And came home with torn clothes and a black eye,
Mrs. Wise would fret: "Fighting . . . just like a nigger!"

If Johnny played "keeps" with hard-boiled boys
And lost his marbles to the gang from an alien street,
The lady would sneer: "Gambling . . . just like a nigger!"

If Johnny failed to study his lessons at night
And brought home low marks on his grade card,
His mother would complain: "Dumb . . . just like a nigger!"

If Johnny attended the highbrow St. John's Church
And fell asleep during a soporific sermon,
The lady would yawn: "Sleeping . . . just like a nigger."

When Mrs. Wise had some of her high-toned friends to tea
And forgot that there was no sugar in the house,
Johnny grinned: "Forgetting . . . just like a nigger."

Willie Byrd

I ain't been no millionaire,
I ain't been no king.
Never been no millionaire,
Never been no king.
When I dies this wicked world
Won't owe me a thing.

I ain't aimin' to git no corns in my hands.
Hard-workin' men die young an' poor.
Constitution of the United States
Guarantees to every man
The rights of life an' the pursuit of what he can git.
So Willie Byrd done spread joy in the forty-eight divisions
An' had two hundred high-steppin' yellah gals.
Fooled with a black woman on Market Street, St. Louis,
An' bad luck followed me for seven years.
Taught me a lesson, though, taught me a lesson.

Fit for Uncle Sam across the pond.
Slipped outa a base hospital one night
An' went down to Paris.
Stayed down there a whole month
Showin' them Frenchmen how to enjoy life.
Got by the officers by sayin':
"Gen'lemen, my mind went a-wanderin'
An' Willie Byrd had to follow his mind."

Better have yo' good times while you kin,
'Cause the graveyard's gonna keep you in.

Won two thousand bucks in a Juarez crap game,
An' had the best-lookin' señorita in the Casino.
Bummed through Ole Mexico 'bout ten months
With Georgia Boy, a deserter from the Tenth Cavalry,
Who soldiered with Pancho Villa.

Georgia Boy was the gamest an' fightingest man
I seen in all my travels.
A little señor in Vera Cruz told me
That Pancho Villa said one time
When Georgia Boy come stridin' into a saloon
Like he owned the world:
"If I wasn't Pancho Villa,
I'd like to be Georgia Boy."

106

Yes, I's sinned every kind of sin . . .
Enjoyed every kind of joy.
After all, my birth was just a accident
That happened to my ma an' pa.
Come into the world with nothin' . . .
Goin' out the same way.

> *I ain't been no millionaire,*
> *I ain't been no king.*
> *Never been no millionaire,*
> *Never been no king.*
> *When I dies this wicked world*
> *Won't owe me a thing.*

Flora Murdock

White Man's proud of bein' white,
Brags about it in de town.
White Man's proud of bein' white,
Brags about it in de town.
White Man oughta shut his mouth
Wid yellah bastards walkin' roun'.

When Flora cooked for old Mrs. Ulma Asch
In Charlotte, North Carolina,
Her flinty-eyed mistress
Nagged her from morning till night
About coming down to work late
And being careless
And running up the grocery bills
And walking on her heels.

If you treat me right, I'll treat you well.
If you treat me wrong, you kin go to hell!

One night
Young Albert Asch,
Who had studied art in Paris,
Returned intoxicated from a church festival
And raped Flora in her bedroom on the second floor.

The girl lost her job,
And old Mrs. Ulma Asch died in a padded cell
Soon after Flora had the abortion.

An itinerant preacher brought Flora to Harlem,
Where she studied under Madame Alpha Devine
And became a famous beauty culturist.

Years later
Flora encountered Albert Asch,
Shabby and half-intoxicated,
At ex-Countess Felicia's studio party
In Union Square.

Albert entertained Flora
With bizarre tales of the Latin Quarter,
And said that she reminded him
Of his mother's high yellow cook
Who was crazy about him down in North Carolina.

108

Maizelle Millay

Hey, pretty Baby,
Each day you's gittin' ol'.
Hey, pretty Baby,
You turned me down fer gol'.
When you cain't shake dat thing no mo',
De men will let you go.
Lawd, Lawd,
De men will let you go.

Maizelle is withered and marred
Like an old potato
Exposed to the whims of the heat and the cold.
Lenox Avenue does not remember the far-off years
When a glimpse of her copperish Creole beauty
Was a breath-absorbing event.

Maizelle's utterance is the croak
Of a thing heard in the empty night.
Lenox Avenue does not remember the far-off years
When her voice was a delicious melody
Floating over the shimmering surface
Of opulent champagne.

Maizelle's body is bent
Like a prairie tree
Under the hurrying feet of the wind.
Lenox Avenue does not remember the far-off years
When her Bayou Passion Dance
Led the revelers captive at the celebrated Plantation Club.

109

Big Fred Railer

Gawd made a man to stand upright
An' look Life in de face.
A henpecked man jest ain't no man,
He's jest one damn disgrace.

Big Fred Railer was the bouncer
At the old Plantation Club.
The wise dopesters said
He would have won the championship of the world
If he'd had the instinct of the killer,
Like Jack Dempsey and Terrible Terry.

Sympathy for an outclassed second-rater
Had been Big Fred's undoing.
Sailor Stein had knocked him cold
When the black giant had slowed up his two-fisted attack;
And the defeat had sent him
To the scrap heap of pugilism.

Big Fred's joviality
Made him a favorite among the nightclub habitués.
He never lost his good humor
When handling the roughest characters.
One night he had to put out
An intoxicated Mississippian,
And the outraged gentleman shot "the black sonofabitch"
In the hip "to teach 'im a lesson."

When Big Fred recovered,
His wife forced him to give up his job
As she had forced him to hang up his gloves.
Willa was haunted ever by the fear
That something would happen to her meal ticket.

110

Like a great Newfoundland,
Big Fred obeyed the mistress of the flat:
He became a janitor in an apartment house;
So that he could be near her.
She was always ailing
And could describe minutely
The shadow of every pain.
Sexually frigid,
She was sure no brute like Big Fred Railer
Could ever understand a sensitive spirit like hers.

One day,
As Big Fred was cleaning under the elevator,
The cage dropped from the top of the shaft
And crushed him to death.

The Stranger

A hongry man wid a empty paw
Will sho' Gawd make or break de Law.

Night came . . . and the fog.
Pedestrians were hurrying ghosts
Beneath half-strangled electric lights.

One great bulb glared
In Mr. Goldberg's pawnshop.
Objects, familiar and bizarre,
Whose secrets would have quickened the heart of Balzac,
Cluttered the ancient shelves and showcases.

As an apologetic elderly gentleman
With a silken white mustache and a classic goatee
Came silently out of the fog,
Mr. Goldberg looked over his glasses and hastened forward,
Rubbing the palms of his greedy little hands.

Mr. Goldberg stopped abruptly
As the stranger aimed at him a small pearl-handled revolver.
"Sir, this pains me very much."
Words polished like an exquisite cameo.

Mr. Goldberg gasped a protest as his hands went above his head,
But the stranger's steely glance sent him straightway
To the cash register
Above which hung a famous reproduction
From the Mannheim Gallery:
The Charlatan.

The gentleman with the classic goatee
Smiled cryptically and exclaimed:
"My countryman, Adriaen Brouwer,
In one of his inspired moments!"

Mr. Goldberg placed the money upon the scarred counter.
The white-haired stranger thanked him
And explained sadly:

"These are the times, Sir,
That try the souls of men . . .
And also their pocketbooks.
Spes sibi quisque."

The stranger backed toward the door,
Slipped the pearl-handled revolver
Into the pocket of his overcoat,
And entered the Harlem fog.

Damon Akerman

What comes after death, no wise man kin tell.
We knows dat on earth some folks catches hell.

I useta hear him upstairs
Whimperin' an' whimperin' an' whimperin'
All night long.
It almost drove me nuts.

Since I was workin' eleven hours a day,
I didn't have to hear him then . . . thank Gawd!
His whimperin' sounded jest like a dawg's I heard oncet
In the Kansas City freight yards
When a switch engine cut off his hind legs.

Sometimes I couldn't stand it a-tall.
So I'd git outa bed
An' go down to Tony the Greek's hole-in-the-wall
An' git a cup of black coffee.

I tell you it almost drove me nuts;
An' I ain't no sissy either,
Havin' served fifteen months on the Western Front.

He was a big strappin' guy, too,
This Damon Akerman . . .
Musta weighed two hundred if he weighed a pound.
He was right young, too,
But his face had wrinkles in it
An' his hair was almost white.
He told me they sometimes git that way in twenty-four hours,
Sufferin' the way he did.

You see, down in Georgia,
He fractured a white man's jaw
When the Cracker pushed his mother off the sidewalk,
An' so they sent him to the chain gang.

The judge said he was a bad nigger.
The judge said if you let these niggers go on
Fracturin' the jaws of white folks
They'd be startin' a Red revolution.

The judge musta told the warden somethin',
For he was always after Damon Akerman.
One day they accused him of gittin' uppity

114

An' placed him between two posts
An' stretched him in the blazin' sun
Till his arms almost come outa the sockets.

After a helluva time Damon reached Harlem.
But rheumatism had settled in his arm sockets.
So I useta hear him upstairs
Whimperin' an' whimperin' an' whimperin',
Jest like that dawg with his legs cut off
Out there in the Kansas City freight yards.
It almost drove me nuts!

Sometimes Aunt Hagar went up to his room
An' rubbed him good with liniments,
An' then his whimperin' didn't sound so gawdamn loud.

The way Damon useta call on the Lawd Jesus Christ,
I don't see how He could keep from
Answerin' his prayers.
Aunt Hagar told me
Man's ways ain't Gawd's ways
An' you have to wait on the Lawd till He's ready,
'Cause Gawd is a busy Gawd
An' He's got millions of things on His mind
In the universe.

One day I was unlockin' my door . . .
I'd jest come home from work . . .
An' Damon was comin' outa his room
With a rope-bound suitcase.
"Leavin', Buddy?" I asked.
He nodded his head
An' said he was goin' back to Georgia . . .
Goin' back to the chain gang.

"I'm goin' to help Gawd do justice," he said.
"I'm goin' to break the sonofabitch
Dat broke me between dem posts!"

I felt cold chills runnin' up an' down my spine;
An' I ain't no sissy either,
Havin' served fifteen months on the Western Front.
I ain't seen nothin' in a guy's eye
Like what I saw in Damon Akerman's.
Give me a cigarette, Black Boy.
Thinkin' about that guy almost drives me nuts!

Black Moses

Any day you may see him on Seventh Avenue,
Black as a jungle night,
His feet unshod,
A looming gray-bearded man,
With frosted shaggy hair.

He carries an ebony staff in one hand
And a large white satchel in the other
On which is printed in Old English letters
"Christ Is Coming! Prepare Ye All!"

The satchel contains pamphlets
On the second advent of the Messiah,
And a passerby can learn all about
The fulfilment of the prophecy
For fifteen cents.

The countenance of Black Moses
Augurs a good nature,
And his voice is like the tone-colors of an organ
In a quiet chapel—
Rich . . . vibrant . . . soothing.

Sometimes he stands hemmed in
By a group of dirty children
Listening, large-eyed and open-mouthed,
To his marvelous stories phrased in simple words.
Sometimes he pauses to soothe troubled old age,
Or to give the manna of sympathy to a cripple.

> You kin fool de ole folks,
>   But I bet a dime
> De kids kin ketch you
>   'Most any ole time.

Pedestrians hail him
Cheerfully,
Respectfully,
As he strides along,
Barefoot,
Unaware of his majestic presence . . .
At peace with God and his fellowmen.

Sometimes a cold-visaged woman of the street,
Or a hawk-eyed loafer at the door of a dive,
Wonders at the benevolent smile
Ever shining
On the unwrinkled face of Black Moses.

116

Uncle Gropper

De Boss he gives a po' hard-workin' man
Some pretty flowers on his funeral day.
De Boss is tryin' to make up fer de times
He didn't pay what he was s'posed to pay.

Uncle Gropper is at rest
After fifty years of toil
From sunup to sundown
On the feudal plantation of Colonel Midas Hooker.

Uncle Gropper was my bosom friend and teacher
In the perilous days of my boyhood.
He taught me to love beauty and truth and fraternity.
Now that the venerable man is dead
I shall catch the first freight train going South.

Everybody in Yazoo County knew Uncle Gropper's melancholy face.
Everybody knew that he saw visions of the last being first.
Everybody knew that bad luck pursued him
Like a bloodhound trailing a barefoot convict.

Colonel Midas Hooker said
Uncle Gropper could plow more furrows in a day
Than any other hand in the Mississippi Delta.
Colonel Midas Hooker said
Watching Uncle Gropper plow
Was like looking at one of Jean Millet's pictures.

Sitting on the porch of his tumble-down cabin
In the soft sheen of the starlight,
Uncle Gropper,
The black Socrates of Yazoo County,
Eyed the furrowy cottonfield across the road
And said to me between puffs of his clay pipe:

"Son, I kin plow through any field Gawd ever made,
But I cain't plow through my debt to Colonel Midas Hooker."

Ain't you tired?
Take yo' rest.
Lay yo' haid on
Jesus' breast.
Lay down, Servant, please lay down,
You done earned yo' heavenly crown.

117

The folks want me to come down there to the funeral.
The folks say the old man called for me
When he died of heart trouble . . .while plowing.

The folks say
Colonel Midas Hooker
Is going to give Uncle Gropper a big funeral
With plenty of condolences
And eulogies
And flowers!

Polly Trotter

> *If you play aroun', Mama, if you play aroun',*
> *Some sweet daddy will sho' Gawd git you down.*

Manhattan Avenue was gray with dawn
When Polly returned from Sylvia's birthday party.
She was seized with a little panic
As her eyes fell upon Bert's long body
Sprawled in a deep armchair . . .
Bert, who'd been too ill to go.

O God, if she hadn't gone to Sylvia's party!
If she hadn't drunk that last cocktail!
If she hadn't taken that last dance with Jazz Boker!

> *If I could read yo' mind, Mama,*
> *Like I read my mail,*
> *Perhaps I'd wanta kill you*
> *An' go to jail!*

Through her gloom she heard Bert breathe her name.
Suddenly he shifted his awkward position,
Opened his eyes, and rubbed the sleep out of them.

She ran to him and flung herself into his arms.
"I missed you so much, Bert! I needed you!"

"Sick or not . . . I'll go with you next time, Honey."
She clutched him convulsively
As the words of Jazz Boker dinned in her brain:
"You're mine now, Baby . . . all mine."

118

Joshua Granite

He has passed the century mark,
This fleecy-haired paralytic
Who lives in everlasting darkness,
His mummy face enslaving the gaze of the passerby
As he sits on the shady stoop
Of the apartment house
Owned by his great-granddaughter.

Stirring events of long ago,
Characters cloistered in history,
Pass in panorama behind his sightless eyes.

He was with Nat Turner of Southampton, Virginia,
That Sunday night in August
When the daring Baptist exhorter and mystic
Began his slave revolt,
Laying waste plantations
And filling the master class with terror.

He was a muleteer in the Union Army
When Sherman marched from Atlanta to the sea . . .
Feasting on chickens and turkeys and ducks,
Feasting on pigs and potatoes and corn.
Old Joshua chuckles when he tells anyone
That was the first time he ever got enough to eat.

He sat in the legislature of South Carolina,
And he trembles with anger
If one speaks slightingly of the black Solons.

The lawgivers were good and bad, ignorant and wise,
In his day as in ours.
Yes, they fixed up the Capitol,
Putting in plate-glass mirrors and lounges,
Desks and armchairs and a free bar;
But they also gave the state a public school system.

Then came the White Scourge,
Ku Klux night riders,
Leaving in their wake burning houses,
Leaving the bodies of carpetbaggers and black freedmen
To give their silent messages
At dawn
From the branches of mutilated trees.

He was at Ogden, Utah, when the golden spike
Of the Union Pacific Railroad was driven.
He was at the open-air meeting in Haymarket Square
When the anarchists clashed with the police.
He was in the May-Day army of Jacob Coxey
When it marched across the lawn of the Capitol.

He has passed the century mark,
This ancient rebel with the mummy face,
Who lives in everlasting darkness with his memories.

Madame Alpha Devine

Madame Alpha Devine she made a million
Straight'nin' out de kinks in woolly hair.
If I had a lotion to turn Black Folks white,
I'd be a billionaire!

Alpha Devine had a vision
Over a steaming washtub on Captain Webb's plantation
At Bitter Ridge, Arkansas . . .
A vision of the Negro Woman Beautiful.

In the Jim Crow cemetery near the Bedrock Baptist Church
She prayed on her mother's sunken grave at midnight;
And a white-robed seraph appeared,
Giving her the formula for the Devine Hair Grower
And commanding her to go into a far city.

The Madame Alpha Devine Manufacturing Company, Inc.,
Has made a fortune for its owner,
Whose business genius established
The Alpha Devine Academy of Beauty Culture,
Which trains colored beauticians.

Black gals use de straight'nin' iron.
White gals use de curlin' rod.
Why cain't folks be satisfied
Wid de handiwork of God?

Madame Alpha Devine goes about the country
In her sumptuous limousine,
Lecturing to worshipping dark ladies.

Madame Alpha Devine tells them
That God has not always blessed her with a mansion on the Hudson,
That she came from the poverty-stricken masses,
That she knows the grime and drudgery of their lives,
That God sent her forth with the Devine Hair Grower
To make kinky hair straight
And short hair luxuriant . . .
The crowning glory of the Negro Woman Beautiful!

Mrs. Edith Parker

What makes me fat
Will make you thin.
What puts me out
Will put you in.
Yea. Ugliness
Is Beauty's twin.

Mrs. Edith Parker. the widow of the great criminal lawyer.
Had four daughters: Clara. Essie. Helen. and Ida.
The first three were beautiful mulattoes.
Images of their mother in her unblemished youth.

Mrs. Parker steered her daughters clear
Of the reefs and shoals of Harlem.
She married Clara to a lawyer.
Essie to a physician.
And Helen to a businessman.

Only Ida was left on Mrs. Parker's hand . . .
Ida. who was the very image of her famous father.
With kinky hair. blossomy lips.
A spreading nose. and a sooty-black face.

Mrs. Edith Parker was distressed . . .
She'd been distressed ever since the birth of Ida.
Yellow women have a ready market among professional men.
But . . . black women . . . ugly black women . . .
Mrs. Edith Parker shuddered.

Ida went serenely on her way.
Unmindful of what she saw in the eyes of her mother and sisters.

Ida married a young preacher
Who said he didn't know what heaven was like
Until he heard the golden voice of Ida
Singing "Swing Low. Sweet Chariot."

The young man's preaching and Ida's singing
Became the seventh wonder of Harlem. . . .
Ten years later. Ida's husband
Stood near the peak of his profession.
He had saved thousands of souls
And built a magnificent temple to the Lord.

The senior bishop said to a high churchman:
"I don't know whether young Graves
Is a man inspired by the Trinity
Or a man enthralled by a woman's voice."

The flowing years bear the flotsam and jetsam of destinies:
Clara had an affair with Dr. Medwick, Essie's husband,
And the crazed wife hurled herself under a subway train;
Helen went to Hollywood,
With Gabby Gay and his Red Hot Rhythm Boys,
To appear in *The Sidewalks of New York*;
And she was last seen, by Sheik Zetkin,
In a Chinese dive of San Francisco.

> *When Life does de Lindy hop,*
> *You may land on de bottom*
> *An' you may land on de top.*

Mrs. Edith Parker suffers
From high blood pressure and hallucinations.

Ida Graves,
Unmindful of the question
She sometimes sees in her mother's eyes,
Goes serenely on her way.

Officer John Cushwa

John Cushwa is the oldest Negro policeman in Harlem.
He is square-shouldered, white-haired, vertical.
Eyes alert, hands expressive,
He directs the school children crossing the street.

A reckless driver stops his truck, grinding the brakes.
Officer Cushwa lumbers forward, his beetle-brows bristling.
"Mister, what's wrong with you?
Wanta run over these kids?
You didn't see my signal?
Let it happen again, an' I'll give you a ticket."

A gay young fellow in a violet-colored roadster
Flashes in from a side street.
A vivid girl snuggles in the curve of his arm.
Laughing roguishly, he pinches her thigh.
"Mister, you must think you're in Lovers' Lane.
This is the second time you've overrode my signal,
An' this is the last warnin'. Get me? Now . . . beat it!"

On the corner of Eighth Avenue is a brazen speakeasy.
A drunkard reels through the door and bumps into a little girl.
She glances up, screams, and scurries up the street.
A serious-faced man walks across to Officer Cushwa.
"Ain't this Prohibition? Why don't you close that dump?"

The square shoulders droop . . . just a little.
Something in the proud figure seems to shrink.
"Mister, I can't do any more about that than you.
I'm just a policeman . . . just a policeman."

Steve Wordsworth

We po' folks in de wilderness
A-wanderin' night an' day.
We po' folks in de wilderness
A-wanderin' night an' day.
We'll jest keep on a-blunderin' round
Until we find de Way.

Night wiped out the gray afternoon
Like an artist erasing a profile.
Opaque figures drifted through the gloom . . .
Dead leaves in a mountain gorge.

Steve Wordsworth, the jobless mechanic,
Came out of the subway,
Tired and hungry and discouraged.
Fifty men representing nine nationalities
Had answered the "ad" for that last job.

He crossed the street to a grubby restaurant.
A gaunt Irishman in greasy overalls
Banged the door open with a crooked arm and strode out.

Steve entered.
The place was alive with fraternizing odors
Of coarse foods and cigarettes and unwashed bodies.
The place was noisy with colliding dishes and uncouth voices.

Steve took a wobbly stool at the bleached counter
And picked up a bespattered menu.
A hard-faced waitress, with a durable figure, approached,
Popping her chewing gum.

"What is it, Mister?" she said carelessly.
Steve replied: "Ham and greens."
The woman relayed the order to a fat-jowled cook
Whose Mephistophelian grin
Filled the small window to the kitchen.

The little rag of a man stood up,
Frantically searching the pockets
Of his slick trousers.
The chill face of the waitress
Tightened with suspicion.

Having found the dime,
He eased it upon the counter,
Wiped his slack mouth on his dingy sleeve,
Pulled his dissenting coat together,
And shuffled backward.

"Thank you, Comrade,"
Said the tall dark stranger
Who took his place.
The little rag of a man said nothing . . .
For in his misery he heard nothing.

Gazing into the cracked mirror behind the counter,
Steve examined the dark features of the man
Whose aristocratic mien
Clashed with the sordid surroundings.

The waitress softened,
And a crafty look in her green eyes fastened itself
Upon the handsome dark face.
When she served him the two doughnuts and coffee,
He said politely: "Thank you."

Turning to Steve, the stranger inquired:
"How are you, Comrade?"
The jobless mechanic eyed him for a moment and gloomed:
"Not so good, Mister. I'm down."

Sympathy shadowed the stranger's face,
But his blue eyes glinted
Like sparks hammered from a steel plate.
"Comrade, the System has pulled us down!
The System holds us down,
Sucking us dry . . . like an octopus!"
The stranger's gesture included the whole place . . .
The whole world.
Steve Wordsworth was puzzled.
"The System?" he echoed. "What system?"

A vast pity flowed into the blue eyes.
Patiently the stranger explained
The mysterious laws back of unemployment.
Steve scratched his head,
His eyes bulging and his mouth agape.

Arm in arm,
The tall dark stranger and Steve left the counter.
The tight-visaged waitress said in a half-whisper:
"The god-damned Red!"

126

Jack Patterson

White boss worked me so damn hard,
Lawd, I couldn't git my breath.
White boss worked me so damn hard,
Lawd, I couldn't git my breath.
Black boss cut my wages down
Till I almost starved to death.

Uncle Rufus,
When I was workin' in a sawmill
Down on the Red River
I heard Steamboat Bill from New Orleans say
When the black boss cut our paychecks:
"Big fish eat up little fish,
An' the color of the fish don't count."

It took me seven years of bummin' around
In America an' China an' Africa an' Europe
To understand what Steamboat Bill was talkin' about.

Uncle Rufus,
This great wide world that God forgot
Opened my eyes!
Seen big yellah fish in Shanghai an' Peking an' Liaoyang
Eatin' up little yellah fish.
Seen big white fish in London an' New York an' Stockholm
Eatin' up little white fish.
Seen big black fish in Addis Ababa an' Monrovia an' Port-au-Prince
Eatin' up little black fish.
So help me God!

The Big Boys in all lands
Give the little fellahs a good shot of dope . . .
The dope of race pride an' patriotism.
Then, while the common people is feelin' big an' dopey,
The Big Boys pick their pockets clean an' call 'em dumb.

Down in Rome, Alabama,
The colored president of Bedrock College
Had a twelve-room mansion an' swell furniture
An' a Packard so long it couldn't turn no corners in town.

The poor white folks got jealous an' full of envy.
A Cracker said to Mayor Hornsby one Saturday night
In the barber shop where I shined shoes:
"Mr. Mayor, it's a goddamn shame!
Why, that black sonofabitch has the finest car
In the whole State of Alabama.
We oughta ride 'im outa town on a L. & N. rail."

Mayor Hornsby winked an' laughed:
"The white race hasta stay on top, don't it?
Well, that nigger president does more
To keep these niggers in their place
Than all the white folks in the State of Alabama;
An', my good man, a servant is worthy of his hire."

Uncle Rufus,
Steamboat Bill knowed what he was talking about:
"Big fish eat up little fish,
An' the color of the fish don't count."

Big Bessie

Black folks sing an' clown an' dance.
Lawd, I wonder why.
Black folks sing an' clown an' dance.
Lawd, I wonder why.
Black folks sing an' clown an' dance
'Cause dey wanta cry.

The Congo Club on Upper Lenox Avenue
Was alive with barbaric splendor,
Its walls vivid with tropical trees
And voluptuous figures in amorous attitudes.
The subdued lights spilled eerie shadows
Over the shuffling dancers and seated carousers.

Sportive waiters with balanced trays
Charlestoned and trucked and Lindy-hopped
Among the smoke-blurred tables.

On a scimitar-shaped platform
Dressed with palms
Gabby Gay and his Red Hot Rhythm Boys
Wailed and blared and quavered mad ecstasies of jazz.

Ain't crazy about money,
Ain't crazy about fame,
But I sho' is wild
About a red hot dame.

A tall, walnut-hued man
Danced with a reddish-brown woman
In a blotch of darkness,
His enormous hands flattened
Against the small of her back.

Her eyes closed,
Her head on his shoulder,
She clasped him convulsively around the neck.
Then, toe to toe,
Feet unmoving,
Their warm bodies rocked and bumped
As they did the Harlem Shake Down.

I ain't no high yellah gal
With blue eyes like the sky.
Ain't no high yellah gal
With blue eyes like the sky.
But my hips is educated,
An' so I's gittin' by.

A looming bouncer
With a livid scar across the crag of his face
Pushed his arrogant way through the crowd.

He tapped the tall, walnut-hued man on the shoulder.
"Git off that dime," the Atlantean bouncer sharped
From the oblique corner of his mouth.

The tune ended in a spasm of tortured harmony;
And the blues-intoxicated couples,
Taking a last fierce hug,
Fell apart,
Laughing deliriously.

I et an' et roast chicken
Until I got enough.
I et an' et roast chicken
Until I got enough.
But I never gits tired of seein'
Big Bessie strut her stuff.

As the dancers drifted to their seats beyond the rails,
A sleek black man
In a form-fitting tuxedo
Walked loftily out and stood
In the center of the dance floor.

He coughed affectedly
Against the back of his hand,
Adjusted his glossy tie,
And clapped for silence.

They say that clothes don't make the man.
Then, Black Boy, tell me why
A well-dressed gent kin always git
A woman's eye.

The yellowish glare of the spotlight
Flashed upon
His mechanical grin and patent-leather hair.

"Ladies an' gen'lemen," he vocalized,
Making a theatrical gesture to the right,
"Permit me to present . . . Miss Bessie Tone . . .
The little lady with the TNT personality
An' the voice that knocks 'em cold . . .
From Harlem to Paris!"

A little rat-faced man
Sitting across from a big-bosomed dark woman
Wisecracked:
"Yeah . . . Paris, Texas!"

> *White gal asked me who I am*
> *In this white man's town.*
> *White gal asked me who I am*
> *In this white man's town.*
> *I'm just an average American gal*
> *Done over in brown.*

A statuesque, sepia-complexioned woman swept forward,
Her jet velvet gown aglow with vari-colored beads.
The announcer bowed extravagantly and shouted:
"Give the little lady a big hand!"

He himself applauded violently,
And from the smoke-veiled tables
Came gusts of hilarity.

At that moment an agitation
Lashed a vague corner of The Congo Club.
A table crashed against the wall,
And chairs tumbled upon the floor.
Above the babel and scuffle
Careered the curse of a man
And the cry of a woman.

"I told dat yellah bitch
To stay away from ma husband!"
Screamed a short, ebony woman
As she snatched up her shabby dress
And whipped out a gleaming razor.

The omnipresent bouncer loomed into view
And gave the ebony wrist a paralyzing wrench.
The razor clattered upon the floor.

He dragged her,
Screeching hysterically,
Toward the front entrance.

"Sing, Big Bessie!"
Shouted the big-bosomed dark woman
Sitting across from the little rat-faced man.

The blues singer nodded graciously,
And her capacious grin revealed
Twin rows of glittering gold.
The Red Hot Rhythm Boys blared a savage chord
And slithered into a lugubrious verse:

> *I know the pangs of grievin'*
> *When you have loved an' lost..*
> *I know men are deceivin'*
> *An' women pay the cost.*

Wiping a tear from her eye
With a small linen handkerchief,
The big-bosomed dark woman leaned
Upon the protesting table and yelled:

"Sing it, Big Bessie!
Sing 'bout these double-faced, lyin' men
That goes around breakin' innocent women's hearts."

She picked up a quart bottle
And took a long, gurgling draught of sloe gin.
Listeners at the neighboring tables guffawed.
The singer's husky voice became tremulous with heartache.

> *But this has been the story*
> *Since history began.*
> *A man loves countless women,*
> *But a woman loves her man.*

The big-bosomed dark woman looked sneeringly
At the little, rat-faced man
Who was giving her fleshy palm
A reassuring pat.

"That's the Gawd's trufe, Big Bessie!
A man ain't nothin' but a low-down dirty dawg
Sweet-daddyin' all the women he kin git . . .
An' a woman loves her only-one man."

> *Daddy, Daddy,*
> *Look what you done to me.*
> *Daddy,Daddy,*
> *Look what you done to me.*
> *You's made me a slave*
> *In de Land of de Free.*

The great dark arm shot out,
Like the enormous reach of a python,
And collared the little, rat-faced man.
Before he could duck,
The Primo Carnera fist crashed against his skull
And he crumpled like a wet dishrag.

"O Lawd Jesus, my sweet daddy's done got hurt!"
She cried, wringing her hands.
"Lawd Jesus, do help my po' little hurt daddy."

The omnipresent bouncer materialized
As a bedlam of merriment engulfed the scene.

> *Black Folks, sing an' dance*
> *De whole night through.*
> *Tomorrow you got White Folks'*
> *Dirty work to do.*
> *But dat won't last always, O Lawd,*
> *Dat won't last always!*

As the hours dragged their weary feet toward dawn,
Fewer and fewer pedestrians were abroad in Lenox Avenue.
But in The Congo Club
The gaiety was mounting
On the wings of wine and song.

A slumming party of whites
From Muskogee, Oklahoma,
Uncomfortably munched their chicken sandwiches
And sipped noisily their sherry.
Big Bessie trucked up to the table
Where they sat pop-eyed and open-mouthed.
Big Bessie sang:

> *Some men like pretty black gals,*
> *An' some men like 'em white.*
> *But, Mister, color sho' don't count*
> *When a gal's in bed at night.*

Mrs. Naomi Sickle,
President of the Foreign Missionary Society
Of the First Baptist Church,
Gaped like a fish out of water and got to her feet.

"The black hussy," she said.
The slumming party of whites
From Muskogee, Oklahoma,
Tugged and stumbled toward the front entrance.
The yellows and browns and blacks belly laughed.

> *From ocean to ocean*
> *My po' feet roam.*
> *When I gits to Nigger Heaven*
> *I's sho' Gawd home.*
> *Lawd, Lawd, Lawd,*
> *I's sho' Gawd home*

Seated at a long table
Containing a small barrel of whiskey,
A half dozen befuddled couples chanted:

> *You think you's something,*
> *But you ain't so hot.*
> *Don't stop your chasin'*
> *Gonna put you on the spot.*
>
> *Tell me how long, Baby,*
> *Do I have to wait.*
> *If you don't hurry up,*
> *Gonna give you the gate.*

A slim pot-black man with a hog-shaped head
Beat out the rhythms on the whiskey barrel
With an empty ginger-ale bottle.

At another table
A bald, amber-hued man
Held a young high yellow girl on his knee,
While she hugged him and kissed his shining pate.
"Take me home, Daddy," she begged. "Take me home."

Black Moses,
Barefoot prophet of the Lord Jesus Christ,
A looming gray-bearded man
With frosted hair and burning eyes,
Entered and surveyed the scene with profound pity.
There was a momentary lull.
He went from table to table with his pamphlets.

134

Came the tone-colors of that organ voice:
"My people dance their way to death
In the black Sodom and Gomorrah.
Christ is coming! Prepare ye all!"

"I got a po' ole mother in heaven!"
Cried the slim pot-black man with the hog-shaped head.
Tears streamed down his face.
"An' a po' ole father in hell.
Christ is comin'! Lawd, have mercy on my soul!"
He slumped upon the table, drunk.

The yellowish spotlight followed Big Bessie,
As her statuesque body swayed in and out
Among the chattering tables.
The jungle ecstasy of Gabby Gay's Red Hot Rhythm Boys
Gloried in blaring gyrations.

Finally Big Bessie stopped before a handsome, nut-brown man
Who gazed at the blues singer
With mocking contempt.
There was a malicious glint in the woman's gray eyes
When she took up the refrain:

> I've got a man who knows his stuff, you see.
> He's got the sugar to sweeten my tea.
> I'm glad you left an' didn't raise a row.
> Your hoop don't fit my barrel nohow!

The nut-brown man sprang like a Bengal tiger
And caught the blues singer by the throat.
He shook her as a dog shakes a rat,
Choking the cry of pain back into her windpipe.

The omnipresent bouncer loomed behind the troubler
And struck him a neat blow behind the ear.
The nut-brown man kneeled over like a careening ship.

Excited onlookers chattered among themselves.
Gabby Gay's Red Hot Rhythm Boys
Let loose a crescendo of crashing notes.
Big Bessie,
Weeping violently,
Floundered through a side entrance marked . . .
The Congo Club.

Ralph Farrell

Ralph Farrell was a near-white
Descendant from Thomas Jefferson.
He was proud of his distinguished ancestry,
But he had a bias for dark beauty in women.

The idea of marrying an octoroon
Came slowly and painfully into his mind
As the years piled up
The little ironies and hypocrisies
Of discrimination and jim crowism in the Democracy
For which his ancestor had signed
The Declaration of Independence.

In the City of Brotherly Love
He took an aristocratic Liberian woman
To a literary dinner for an old classmate,
The winner of a Pulitzer prize.

The frightened hotel clerk sent for the manager,
Who blandly explained:
"No Negro guest has ever been served in this hotel.
I regret that we cannot accommodate the lady."

At the San Diego International Exposition
Farrell entered a café with a dark woman,
And a red-necked waiter from Mississippi sputtered:
"We don't serve . . . er . . . Nigroes.
Of course, Mistah, you can eat here,
But—" He glanced significantly at the dark woman.

New York is a liberty-loving commonwealth.
She has no segregation laws
Like the cultural Sahara of Mississippi.

One evening Farrell went to a restaurant near Carnegie Hall
With a golden-brown singer
Whose genius had favored European royalty.

The waiters, making much ado about nothing,
Kept them waiting an hour.
Then it took five waiters two hours
To serve the dinner.
The guests were dismayed to discover
Their coffee was bitter with salt.

136

The years piled up
Little ironies and hypocrisies
Of discrimination and jim crowism in the Democracy
For which his ancestor had signed
The Declaration of Independence.

Ralph Farrell married a near-white,
And they starred themselves in *The Comedy of Passing*.

They stayed in white hotels in Atlanta and Memphis.
They were the guests of white friends
In Dallas and Birmingham and Richmond.
They rode in Pullman coaches through the Bible Belt
And stayed in tourists' camps . . .anywhere.

They flirted with Negrophobes
And then disclosed their racial identity.

They did the Yazoo Bump and the Georgia Jelly Roll
And advocated miscegenation
In the presence of panicky white respectables.

They told how a Southern gentleman
Of Tazewell County, Virginia,
Kept four Negro women for each of his three sons
To breed beautiful mulatto girls for the market.

They asked white Christian clergymen
What kind of sermon Jesus Christ would preach
In a jim crow church.

They told vivid tales about
The vitalizing masculinity of black men
And the rejuvenating passion of dark women.

"You've not lived until you've had a black lover,"
Sighed Mrs. Ralph Farrell among gaping white ladies.

"I never dreamed what love was like
Until I took a Negro woman,"
Chuckled Mr. Ralph Farrell
As white gentlemen stared over their cocktails and cigars.

One summer they took a course in anthropology
At a famous Southern university.

They pilloried their celebrated professor
With questions on the problems of race
And startling revelations in Negro history.

Traveling from Richmond in a drawing room,
The Governor said to his guest from New York:
"Mr. Farrell, you can always tell a nigger
By the color of his finger-nails and the odor of his body."

Ralph Farrell laughed until the tears came.
Then he clapped the Governor on the back.
"You're a great wit, Your Excellency," he said.

Pastels

Jesse Seegar

The New Year comes, the Old Year goes.
What's down the road nobody knows.
I play my suit with a poker face,
But Father Time he holds the ace.

Harlem was ushering in the New Year.
Merrymaking crowds zigzagged through the streets.
Wild-eyed boys banged out crazy rhythms
On boxes and buckets and cans.
Taxicabs sent breakers of honking frenzy
Crashing against scabrous walls.
Now and then whistles jackknifed
Through the delirium of sound.

Met a Creole woman
Down in New Orleans.
Sweet, sweet Creole mama
Down in New Orleans.
Creole woman stole my heart
With her conjure beans.

Jesse Seegar elbowed his way along Seventh Avenue.
"I'm turning over a new leaf," he reassured himself.
"I'm leaving Lovie Lovelace alone for good."

Old Samson he was big an' strong,
But let a woman git 'im wrong.
Just keep a level head, you fool;
Then you won't be no woman's tool.

The sidewalk in front of the Lafayette Theatre was jammed.
Seegar stepped on the corns of a big-bellied yellow man.

Seegar apologized effusively
As the stranger groaned:
"You blind bastard!"

Then tinkled the silver dinner bell
Of a woman's clear, fragile laughter.
A familiar hand clasped his arm.
Seegar's heart fluttered like a frightened hen.

"Sweetheart," dimpled the woman,
And the large black eyes vivified
The russet-tinted face.

Jesse Seegar said breathlessly:
"Lovie Lovelace . . . I . . .
I didn't expect to see you here."

They disappeared in the dusky tide
That swirled along Seventh Avenue.

> *What does it matter? You an' I*
> *Are like the dead leaves driftin' by.*
> *I play my suit with a poker face,*
> *But Father Time he holds the ace.*

Dave Zachary

Why will a dawg leave one good bone
To git another bone?
Why don't a woman wid one good man
Leave other men alone?

The big-bellied yellow man limped
Toward the door of The Zachary Eat Shop.

Breathing a sigh of relief, he entered his domain.
"Hello, Zachary," came a din of voices.
Flashing a gold-toothed grin,
He gave a half-military salute
And rocked toward the table where his wife sat,
Her chin resting on her cupped palm.

"Hello, Honey," He patted the velvety brown hand
Bediamonded with miniature constellations.
She drawled: "You got here at last."
He slumped into a seat and grimaced:
"After a damn nigger almost ruined my feet."

She frowned: "I'm tired as hell, Dave."
After a pause, he suggested:
"You better turn in early, Honey. You've had a hard day."

He escorted her to the door. "Good night," he said.
She pecked him on the cheek and joined the upgoing crowd.

In front of the Lafayette Theatre
A dusky Beau Brummel laughed:
"I thought you'd never come, Precious."

Her hazel eyes answered him
With a passionate gleam.

If a woman wants another man,
There's nothing you kin do,
But look around to find someone
Who wants a man like you.

Hailing a taxicab,
He guided her to the curb.
To the driver he said:
"Jazz Boker's Place on Strivers' Row."

143

Tubby Laughton

Mind yo' business, Black Boy,
An' we will git on fine.
I may not want you, Black Boy,
To help me handle mine.

Harlem was ushering in the New Year.
A taxicab stopped in front of The Zachary Eat Shop.

Tubby entered the café with a purposeful stride.
A white-jacketed West Indian stood near the door.

Tubby hesitated. "Where's Zachary?" he queried.
The West Indian barked: "At the last table on the right."

The top of the table was hidden
By dishes swollen with food.
Dave Zachary's beefy head hung low over an enormous platter
Glutted with porterhouse steak.

Tubby's little eyes gleamed with greed.
The big-bellied yellow man looked up . . .
Very much like a hog disturbed at its trough.
Zachary back-wiped his mouth. "Well?" he snorted.

"One good turn deserves another," Tubby said.
"Mr. Zachary, I just drove Mrs. Zachary an' a strange man
To Jazz Boker's Place on Strivers' Row."

Dave Zachary's huge fist struck like a trip-hammer.
Tubby spun crazily on his heels and toppled sideways.
As two waiters carried the inert body through the front door,
Dave Zachary's teeth sank into a piece of juicy steak.

144

Crip Mackay

> *I may have to go to hell to live*
> *Wid Satan an' my po' ole Pa.*
> *But I's gonna keep my pot-black self*
> *Outa de State of Arkansas.*

Harlem was ushering in the New Year.
In the Four Square Barber Shop, four figures,
Indistinct like twilight, blurred the chairs
Facing the cracked mirrors across the room.

Crip MacKay stretched his long, lean legs.
"This time last year," he said,
"I was in a boxcar in Arkansas,
Bummin' my way back to Harlem.
Ever been to Arkansas?
Well, the white folks down there are harder on niggers
Than Jack Johnson was on Jim Jeffries.

"I was behind an empty piano box, hidin'.
The freight pulled upon a sidin'
To wait for the Memphis Yellah Dog to pass.

"I was layin' on my back dreamin' about Harlem
When the door opened an' I saw in the moonlight
A white woman climbin' into the car.
Another Scottsboro case! I thought.

"Fear growed in me till it puffed out my skin.
The woman was talkin' . . . talkin' to herself.
'O God, if I hadn't done it!' she kept sayin'.

"The door was open; the moon bright as day.
Once I thought I'd better git off,
For if the cops—
Well, I wouldn't be tellin' it now.
Then somethin' told me to lay low;
'Cause if the woman knowed I was there—
Well, I decided to lay low.

" 'O God, if I hadn't done it!' The woman kept sayin'.
Then she broke down an' started cryin' an' prayin'.
Ain't that somethin'? A poor white woman an' a poor nigger
In a boxcar down in Arkansas, an' both prayin',
As the freight clips off fifty-five.

"Suddenly the woman got to her feet, yellin'.
Ain't heard nothin' like it even in no-man's-land.
Then she began whimperin':
'Hiram, don't touch me.
Don't touch me, Hiram.
Your brother made me poison you.
I didn't want to do it, Hiram.
Honest to God . . . I didn't!'

"It was awful, men, awful.
I had to put my hands to my ears
To keep from screamin' out.
Have you ever seen a woman's soul, bare, bleedin'?

"A funny thing happened to me.
I'd always hated white people.

I'd always rejoiced when whites were killed
In storms an' floods an' wrecks. The hand of God, I said.
You see the white militia had murdered my brother
In the race riots in East St. Louis.
Yes, a funny thing happened to me, in that boxcar.
The walls of the prison of race hate
Pushed out . . . out . . . an' left me free.
I forgot the woman was white
An' remembered she was a woman . . .
A woman who needed help.

"The woman was swayin' crazily on her feet.
Her hair was hangin' down.
The freight was movin' along at about fifty-five.

"Suddenly the woman screamed, whirled about,
Ran to the open door, an' jumped.

"I heard nothin'
But the clickety-clack, the clickety-clack, of the rails.
I saw nothin'
But the moon shinin' through the open door."

Elbert Hartman

Says I to myself: Gonna be myself,
Enjoy my democracy.
Lawd, I looks funny to some white folks
An' dey looks funny to me.

Harlem was ushering in the New Year.
The famous literary critic, Elbert Hartman,
Was showing his guests the nightlife of Harlem.
They wanted to see Nigger Heaven.
They wanted to tell their Boston friends about Nigger Heaven.

Breasting the colorful crowds,
Hartman was kept busy answering questions
About the primitive Negroes,
The quaint Negroes,
The happy-go-lucky Negroes.

Mrs. Gene Mortimer inquired archly:
"My dear Mr. Hartman, am I to understand
There are Negro poets and novelists in Harlem?"
Hartman's eyes twinkled.

As he evaded a fat dark woman
With a vast shopping basket on her arm,
He pointed his cane across the street.
"See that church on the corner?"
The group pressed toward the curb.

Hartman explained: "The father of Countee Cullen,
A brilliant young Negro poet, is its pastor."

The group craned their necks and tittle-tattled excitedly.
Hartman continued: "The poet and his father live next door.
I've been there many a time. Cullen is a wonderful fellow."

Mrs. Gene Mortimer elevated her lorgnette.
"That's quite intriguing," she said. "A Negro poet!"

A thin black woman passed with her dapper sweet man.
She giggled: "What's dat ofay got against her eyes?"
The man grinned; "Damned if I know!"
The couple laughed brazenly
As the dusky flood sucked them in.
Hartman hid his smile behind a gloved hand.

They approached the Lafayette Theatre.
Mr. Dresbach whispered to Mrs. Gene Mortimer;
"This looks like Africa on parade!
Did you ever see so many different kinds of niggers?"

"Judge Byrd," said the old banker, "I can't explain it,
But I feel younger. This street is alive! It's vital!"

Mrs. Gene Mortimer
Gave her husband a reproving glance.
"The closer one approaches the primitive,"
She elucidated in her platform manner,
"The greater the vitalism."

The old banker chuckled . . .
And straightened his shoulders.
The lady sniffed disdainfully
Like a peerless Pekingese.

> *Dat high-hattin' mama holds her head so high*
> *She don't see de black hearse a-rollin' by.*

"This is the Tree of Hope," said Hartman,
Rubbing his fingers against the scarred trunk.
"Harlemites say it'll give you good luck.
It's changed the destinies of actors and singers,
Of prizefighters and politicians and lovers.
Some say it brought good luck to Richard B. Harrison
And Bojangles Robinson and Paul Robeson.
The Tree of Hope has an illustrious history."

Little Miss Mildred Mortimer stroked the tree
With her pink white fingers.
"Mildred!" cried her horrified mother,
Raising her lorgnette sharply.
"Why, one would think you a superstitious darky."

Overhearing Mrs. Gene Mortimer's remark,
An angular black woman glared at her.

The lady nervously tapped the lorgnette
On her fleshy white palm.
"I've seen enough of Harlem," she grimaced.

The others did not hear her.
They were listening to Hartman's anecdote
About Flo Ziegfeld and Bert Williams
And the Tree of Hope.

Festus Conrad

The fugitive returned on New Year's Eve
From the Brazilian plantation where he had worked
Since his escape
From a federal officer in a Texas jim crow car.

His mother's body,
Covered with a frayed blanket,
Formed a narrow mound in the bed.
On each side, exposed,
Lay the fleshless brown arms and the stiff fingers
That would never again beat out staccato rhythms
On the ribbed keys of washboards.

Festus looked at his mother's head,
Amazingly small,
Shrunk by poverty and worry and disease.

Pity touched the quick of his heart,
And a cold chill laid its hand upon him,
And his mind wavered on the brink of chaos.

In the room of death memories tiptoed by,
And in the night, as the old year ebbed into oblivion,
A strange peace entered the door of his being,
Followed by a vivifying joy.

His mother was free!
Free from washtubs in damp basements,
Free from poverty and worry and disease,
Free from the ball-and-chain of circumstance!

Bowyer Bragg

Dat man could look you in de eye
An' tell de damnedest kind of lie.
De man was borned to lie, but we
Just liked to hear his lies, you see.

Gen'lemen, here we is in the Four Square Barber Shop,
But on last New Year's Eve
I was at a rent party on Upper Lenox.
Ole friend of mine throwed it an' begged me to come.
Said he'd have some good-lookin' gals
Who was crazy to meet Mr. Bowyer Bragg.

I meets a chocolate-brown Mae West, Gen'lemen,
Who falls for me like a ton of bricks.

> *You wonder why all the women fall for me.*
> *It's the TNT in my personality.*

I starts dancin' with this hip-teasin' mama,
An' we jelly-rolled just like we'd been borned together.
About three A.M. I takes her home.

I was sittin' there, legs crossed, smokin', homelike,
An' she was comminglin' two highballs in the kitchen.
A key turned in the lock—an' so help me God!—
In walked the biggest, blackest, ugliest, meanest nigger-man
That God Almighty ever messed up on one of His off-days.

He said nothin', and' I said nothin'.
I just sat there, calm, cool, an' collected.
Gen'lemen, my conscience was clear as a new-borned babe's.

> *A righteous man needs no defense!*
> *Dat's sho' one lie dat don't make sense.*

"Good evenin'," I says like one gen'leman to another.
He stared at me . . . an' through me.
"Are you lookin' for the lady of the house?" I asked, pleasantlike.

At that he begun swellin' up,
Just like a big cobra swellin' up.
Then he starts movin' toward me . . .
Somethin' like Jack Dempsey shufflin' in to make a kill.

150

The woman's voice comes from the kitchen, lovelike:
"Make yourself at home, Sweetie.
Dad's gone for a long time."

Daddy-man lunges at me like a mad bull.
I jumps upon the bed an' goes over the side.
I reaches the door an' the head of the steps
As his ungodly foot catches me in my caboose.
The dynamite in that daddy-man's toe
Musta jarred all my kinfolks in Kentucky.

I spent New Year's Day in the Harlem Hospital.
A few days later I saw the woman on Seventh Avenue.
Her face looked like a strip of no-man's-land.
"Hello, Sweetie," she said. "Come up an' see me sometime."

I eyed her caboose an' lifted my foot . . .
But Officer 999 come outa Tony the Greek's place.

Winged Feet Cooper

In the stage section of the New York *Times*
Lula Mae showed Buck
The black-and-white study of Winged Feet Cooper,
Whose acrobatic tap dancing had spired him
From the beggarly sidewalks of Harlem
To fame and fortune in the capitals of Europe.

"Just think," exclaimed Lula Mae,
"Once he asked me to marry him!"

Thereafter the ghost of Winged Feet Cooper
Haunted the McKinney household,
And the erstwhile jolly Buck
Felt the noose of inferiority tighten about his neck.

Lula Mae's scrapbook contained pictures
Of the celebrated dancer in notable poses.
Proudly displaying these before her friends,
She embellished the career of her former admirer.
"Cooper was so much in love with me," she sighed.

Buck and Lula Mae used to attend the Savoy,
But now he stubbornly refused to go,
Imagining himself as graceful in a ballroom
As a truck horse in the Kentucky Derby.

New Year's Eve, Winged Feet Cooper
Came to the Harlem Opera House.
Lula Mae was breathless with expectancy.

She bought the most fashionable gown
In the Harlem Shoppe,
And drew Buck's last dollar from the bank to pay for it.

Buck sweated from humiliation
When she made him struggle into the tuxedo
She'd rented from Mr. Goldberg.

In the august box at the Harlem Opera House,
Buck sat like a stuffed owl
While Lula Mae scanned the vast audience
With the opera glass rented from Mr. Goldberg.

Buck's discomfort mounted like a fever,
When the dapper Winged Feet Cooper
Glided upon the stage
And the applause of the spectators
Roared like a cannonade.

Buck sickened with disgust
When Lula Mae leaped to her feet
And clapped her hands and chirped her ecstasy.

"Buck," said Lula Mae, "isn't he a dear?
We must meet him backstage."

They went down the alley to the stage entrance,
But the giant doorman wouldn't let them in.
Outside, they waited and waited.
By twos and threes,
Actors drifted from the cavernous doorway
Into the Harlem fog.

Winged Feet Cooper
Emerged finally
With a beautiful octoroon clinging to his arm.

Lula Mae was taken aback,
But hastily she nerved herself and stepped forward.
"I just had to see you, Jimmy," she broke out.

The dancer glanced at her sharply,
Without a scintilla of recognition.
"Don't run over us, Sister," he protested.
Then turning to the puzzled octoroon, he explained:
"These stage-door dames are a plague."

Lula Mae, faint from humiliation,
Braced herself against the chilly wall.
Like one coming out of a bad dream,
She looked around for her support
In times of trouble:
The tall figure was a blur in the distance.

"Buck!" she cried. "Buck!"
Out of the hostile fog came an unreal voice:
"I don't play second fiddle for nobody."

Nutty Al Moon

The crazy thing Al Moon did
Elicited the nickname Harlem gave him.
Miss Eulaline Briffault whispered to the Paul Benefields,
At a meeting of the Harlem Book Lovers' Club,
That Catherine had made Al what he was.
The most successful businessman on Seventh Avenue
And president of the Harlem Chamber of Commerce.

When Catherine married Al,
He was a nobody and his parents were nobodies
Who collected rags and junk from janitors.
Catherine took the profits from her beauty shop
And set Al up in business.

Rung by rung, she pushed Al up the ladder,
And when he slipped—
Al's slips were astonishingly frequent and perilous—
Catherine propelled him upward religiously . . .
And everybody who was anybody in Harlem saw her do it.
Did not the Reverend Paramount Dana say as much
In his famous sermon, "The Duties of Good Wives"?

Now, when the Al Moons had become
What Mrs. Catherine Moon wanted them to be in Harlem society
Her husband disappeared one night
Like a pebble
Dropped into the cavernous throat of a well.

Negro newspapers featured pictures
Of the Al Moons on their honeymoon
In Atlantic City.
Two or three reporters found signs
Of kidnaping and foul play.

Napoleon Hannibal Speare thundered in *The Harlem Advocate*:
"Italians Try to Oust Negro Businessmen!
Case of Alfred Moon Proves Necessity of Race Unity!!!"

Mrs. Catherine Moon basked in the publicity
Like a dog sunning itself on a congenial doorstep.

A week later
A detective discovered Al Moon
Living in Greenwich Village with Ann Hudd, a chorus girl
From The Harlem Blackbirds.

154

The headline of *The Harlem Advocate* screamed:
"Alfred Moon's Bohemian Love Nest Shocks Harlem Society!"

Sister Cripens said Al was crazy as a june bug . . .
Leaving a good woman like Catherine in these hard times
To live with a whore
Who would give him all he wanted for a dollar.
Mother Vibbard stopped smoking her clay pipe
Long enough to inform her daughter:
"A dawg will go back to his vomit."

Miss Eulaline Briffault said:
"I can sympathize with you, Mrs. Moon.
However, I thought at the time
You were making a tragic mistake
In marrying below your social level.
Don't worry, my dear,
Alfred Moon will come crawling back to you,
And then . . . then . . ."
Miss Eulaline Briffault, departing,
Left a malicious imp of laughter capering in the room.

Walking up Lenox Avenue
The night before Christmas,
Catherine saw Al and the chorus girl come out of a store,
Laughing like two mischief-making children.
The chorus girl had an armful of Christmas packages.
Al was swaggering with a baby carriage.

The *Harlem Advocate* carried a red streamer:
"Prominent Businesswoman Has Nervous Breakdown From Overwork!"

Harold Lincoln

His Harlem intimates will tell you
He has a brilliant mind,
But he's a misfit.

He has been a teacher,
A newspaperman, a groceryman,
A bank clerk, a superintendent,
A song writer, and a policeman.

He was born and reared in Coffeyville, Kansas.
His father the son of a slave
Who escaped from Kentucky
By way of the Underground Railroad.

When his country entered the World War,
Harold Lincoln was doing graduate work
In an eastern university.
Aroused to patriotic endeavor,
He entered the training camp for colored officers
At Des Moines, Iowa,
And came out a second lieutenant.

His series of disillusions began
With the discovery of the antagonism of white soldiers
Toward commissioned black officers.
But the inspiriting cry,
"Make the world safe for democracy,"
Sent him to France with upleaping hopes.

Over there,
He found that white Americans
Tried to discredit their colored comrades
In the eyes of French soldiers and civilians.
He saw Negro soldiers assigned to coaling and stevedore work.
He saw Negro officers humiliated.
And in the hell of no-man's-land
His dream of democracy became one with the rot and the stench.

He fought . . . not knowing why . . .
And was wounded four times.

Interminable days and unending nights,
He lay in a base hospital, his body twisted and his mind twisted.
He received two medals for gallantry in battle . . .
Medals that irony pinned on the breast of a dead German.
Arrested one night for talking to a French woman,
He insulted a high officer and was court-martialed.

His Harlem intimates will tell you
He has a brilliant mind,
But he's a misfit.
He has gone from job to job and from city to ciy,
Seeking something he cannot find.

At different times he has been a follower
Of Nietzsche and Jesus and Marx . . .
He is now a nihilist
Married to a Bronx Jewess and working as a redcap.

Ray Rosenfeld

Blond and needy and eager,
Ray Rosenfeld sat in the palatial office
Of America's best-selling magazine.
Behind an ornate desk;
The elephantine body of the spectacled editor
Stirred in an enormous chair.

"Well, Rosenfeld," said Mr. Edwin Kennedy,
Without removing his formidable cigar,
"The country is raving about Harlem.
I want you to spend a whole week up there
And get the lowdown on Nigger Heaven.
Our readers like spicy stuff. See?"

Ray Rosenfeld visited the black Mecca
And took notes on exotic characters and places;
Then using his fecund imagination,
He wrote a series of articles
On the cabaret habitués and the messiahs,
The rent parties and the policy rackets,
The speakeasies and the new religions,
The nigger-chasers and the dirty sweet men.

Mr. Edwin Kennedy was vastly pleased with the work.
He gave Rosenfeld one of his formidable cigars
And patted him on the shoulder.

Then Mr. Kennedy called in Billy Warner,
The dreamy reefer-smoking artist from Mobile,
Who had lived around black folk all his life;
In his hands Mr. Kennedy placed the task
Of making exotic illustrations.

Ray Rosenfeld's colorful articles
Reached the remote corners of the earth.
Persons of every race and every clime
Laughed at the expense of Harlem,
Felt superior at the expense of Harlem.
They talked glibly about the jungle dances,
The jungle passions, the jungle rhythms,

The jungle laughter, the jungle religions.
And . . . above all . . . the jungle ways of making love.

The Committee on Public Morals
Thanked Mr. Ray Rosenfeld for his investigations,
And descended on Harlem like the seven plagues of Egypt.

Harlemites winked at each other
And devised bizarre ways of entertaining
The crowds of Caucasians who came Uptown
Seeking an escape from civilization.
Cabarets introduced the jungle atmosphere.
Finding that Satan had a stronger following than God,
Many of the churches tried to beat Satan at his own game,
By jazzing the spirituals and hiring hip-shaking evangelists.

Whirlwind Cotton

Whirlwind Cotton started as an amateur
At the Kansas City Athletic Club
On Deep Eighteenth.

One night Mike Furman sat at the ringside
And saw the youngster swing into action
With that cyclonic, two-fisted attack:
And the gray wizard perceived the divine stuff
Of which great champions are made.

Mike Furman guided Whirlwind
Along the mazy trail that led to the door
Of Jack Lombardo, the lightweight champion of the world.

As the day of the fight drew near,
The betting odds tilted in Whirlwind's favor.
Sports writers never grew weary of describing
The two-fisted onslaught of the ebony Cotton.
A veteran who had followed the ring for forty years
Dubbed him The Waltzing Slugger.
One-Eye Conroy ranked him above Joe Gans.

It was late afternoon in the fall.
Mike and Whirlwind walked along the flat beach
Bordering Atlantic City.
The gray-haired little master was inspiring his pupil
With the dramatic lore
Garnered during his checkered career as a manager.

Mike stopped suddenly
And placed his hand on Whirlwind's shoulder,
Beyond them
The bluish-gray waters tumbled shoreward
And sea gulls slanted downward in the setting sun.

"Whirlwind," said old Mike, "I've taught you every trick
In the game, and I've staked everything on you."

Cotton's eyes grew misty like a child's.
He grasped Mike's hand.
"I'm goin' in there tomorrow night," he choked,
"To win fer you an' the madam."

160

The fans were packed in Madison Square Garden
Like sardines in a can.
When the two fighters and their retinues swung down the aisle,
The historic walls and corridors
Reverberated with hand clapping and lusty shouts. . . .

Ring followers still argue
About that disappointing fight
In which Cotton was more like a zephyr
Than a whirlwind.
Gone was the rhythm of his cyclonic, two-fisted attack,
As the jeering champion belted him about the ring.

The ebony challenger buckled and cowered and bicycled away,
His face a gory fantasy.

A giant black man with a bullet head
Took a long drink from a quart flask and yelled:
"The yellah sonofabitch!"

A little Italian in a checkered suit,
Crushed his cigarette butt under his heel
And said out of the corner of his mouth:
"Whirlwind's off tonight
The best of 'em have a night off."

The giant black man with the bullet head
Glared at the little Italian:
"The sonofabitch's night off
Is puttin' me off all ma dough fer the wintah."

Mike Furman was frantic.
The hisses and jeers of the crowd
Seeped into his ears like drops of acid.
Between rounds
He cursed and prayed and begged and wept.
His words fell upon Whirlwind
Like hail beating upon the insensible roof
Of a Harlem tenement.

Then the referee raised the champion's swarthy hand
At the end of fifteen tragic rounds
And the deafening roar crashed about the ring,
A broken old man climbed through the ropes
And threw a fatherly arm around the sagging shoulders
Of the ghastly challenger.

161

That night Mike and Whirlwind
Walked the silent streets:
Whirlwind, heart weary because he had disappointed
The little master;
The old white man patient because he was trying
To discover a secret.

At last Whirlwind broke down
And stammered out the story
Of how he had slipped off to Harlem that afternoon
To get his good-luck rabbit foot
And found his wife in bed
With Blue Finch, the tap dancer.

"Brace up, Whirlwind," said Mike,
A sudden joy brightening his face and voice.
"Brace up. I'm satisfied now.
I knew that mug couldn't whip you!"

But Whirlwind said gloomily:
"One thing puzzles me:
How could ma rabbit foot bring me such bad luck?"

Big Shot Lacy

His father was a Baptist preacher,
The years of his service to God being thirty-six,
The number of his children fourteen,
His income and possessions spiritual.

Going to bed with half enough to eat,
Going to school and to church half-clothed,
Little Lacy grew into boyhood
Hating poverty with an implacable hatred.

"When I become a man," he said,
"I'm going to have plenty of money.
I'm going to eat and dress like other people.
Dad makes me sick, praying and singing
While mother works herself to death."

The night his mother died of childbirth,
The crowded flat was filled with wailing.
Three or four preachers came in
And added their prayers to the Reverend Lacy's.

Little Lacy sat clear-eyed,
Holding his mother's cold fingers
And looking at her small face,
Tranquil in death.
The old clock on the mantlepiece
Struck the hour of twelve.
He got up and left the flat,
Never to return.

Big Shot Lacy is king of the Harlem Bolito racket.
He operates seven speakeasies
He owns the Panama Club
Where Big Bessie sings the latest hit,
"I've Got a Man."
He owns the Harlem Palace
Where the biggest chances are stages.
He has social prestige
Since his marriage to Elizabeth Canby,
And the politicians pat him on the back.

Two sharp-eyed ebony giants
Accompany him everywhere,
One in front and the other behind.
"I may not live long," says Big Shot Lacy,
"But I'm living while I'm living."

Percy Longfellow

I have slept on the fragrant breasts of oases.
Under the sheen of the stars.
I have romanced with the virgin plains of the West
In the cool of refreshing dawns.

I have dreamed by the side of mountain streams,
Bewitched by the cadence of rippling silver.
I have listened to the love songs of moss-draped oaks
On the banks of darkling bayous.
I have pillowed my feverish head
On the dusky lap of the Gulf Stream.

Intoxicated by siren kisses.
I have been dragged down and down
By the passion of the Tropics.

I have held many a tryst with far-flung hills
That embraced me with arms of solitude.
I have been the paramour of the brazen North,
And exhausted by the excesses
Of her unappeased appetite.

I have loved chaste villages and buxom towns.
I have been enamored of voluptuous cities.

Having known so many loves since I left you,
Returning to you,
O Harlem,
Mistress of my youth . . .
I know now what the supreme love is.

Sterling the Artist

Gray tatters of smoke floated lazily above the tables
Where the parties made merry in the Dixie Club.
A coal-black entertainer in red chiffon velvet
Undulated to the center of the dance floor and crooned:

The black widow spider
Gets rid of her man,
Gets rid of her daddy
As fast as she can.
If you hang around
I know what I'll do,
Like the black widow spider
I'll get rid of you.

The Dixie Club became a topsyturvydom of laughter and applause.
Jaws hard-set under the bronzy skin, eyebrows drawn close,
Smoke from a cigarette spiring above his long fingers,
The earnest words of the artist drifted across the highball glasses
The oval-faced cream-complexioned woman
Crowned with a shining rope of black hair—
The woman whose vanity had cursed him and his art.

Some women live happy
With only one man.
That's okay I reckon . . .
Be damned if I can.

The bronze-colored man leaned forward, every muscle taut.
His deep eyes held the fierceness of a caged animal's.
His thin lips were chiseling the words
With the pitiless precision of a cutting tool.

The eyes of the cream-complexioned woman flashed
Like twin lights dissecting a lake at midnight.
With a definitive gesture
She drew her golden evening cloak about her ivory shoulders . . . .

The bronze-colored man sat alone, hands clasped upon the table.
The coal-black entertainer in the red chiffon velvet
Undulated toward him and paused to croon:

The black widow spider
Gets rids of her man,
Gets rid of her daddy
As fast as she can.

The bronze-colored man tossed the entertainer a dollar bill.
She nodded acceptance and gave him a half-smile.

165

Doctor James

Doctor James is recuperating
In the bachelor apartment
Of his old friend, Dr. Harvey Whyte.

When he recovers from his injuries,
He's going to bring his family from Washington, D.C.,
And practice his profession in Harlem.

Two months ago, Doctor James was suffering,·
In the capital, from influenza;
And, while confined to his bed,
He received a telegram from Atlanta, Georgia,
Saying his mother was dying and wanted to see him.

Doctor James went to a white physician,
Who'd been his classmate in the medical college,
And had him secure a ticket
With Pullman accommodation.

By staying in his drawing room, with the shades drawn,
And tipping the race-proud porter,
He reached Atlanta safely.

The old woman died happy
In the arms of her eldest son.

On his return,
At midnight the train stopped at a small town.
A group of masked men brushed the Pullman porter aside
And took Doctor James from his berth.

One of the hooded night riders said:
"You're one of them smart niggers.
We'll teach you a lesson you won't fergit."

Shivering in his pajamas,
Doctor James heard the lonesome whistle of the train
As it sped toward the North.

166

They took him across the tracks
To the Negro section of the town.
In front of a rickety Negro church,
They tarred and feathered him.
Then they beat him methodically
And left him to die.

Later, an Amazonian black woman,
With an ugly scar on her left cheek,
Lumbered up the church steps.
She picked up the unconscious traveler
And carried him to her shack
As if he were an infant.

Her vile curses filled the dingy street
As the whites of eyes gleamed
Behind parted window curtains . . . .

Sometimes Doctor James catches Dr. Harvey Whyte
Watching him with melancholy eyes.
But you never can tell what Dr. Harvey Whyte is thinking.

Judge Crimpton

The old gentleman entered the Harlem Meat Market;
With difficulty he closed the door
Against the wintry blast that pushed him in,
And about his long legs
Billowed his threadbare overcoat.

His knee joints ached
As he walked stiffly toward the rear counter,
Attempting to carry himself with dignity.
His fading distinction
Held a little of the ludicrous and the pathetic,
And his watery eyes blinked painfully
While he stood under the glaring bulb.

"What is it, Judge?" chuckled the butcher,
Wiping his stubby red fingers on the white apron
Ballooned at his aggressive paunch.
The old gentleman hesitated, then stammered:
"I want some scraps . . . some scraps for my dog.
He's hungry, very hungry, Mr. Goodwin."

Still chuckling, the butcher picked up, here and there
Scraps of meat from the huge round blocks.
Judge Crimpton stood before the long shining showcase
In whose white trays lay juicy steaks and roasts.
Slowly a wolfish gleam came into the human eyes,
And the old gentleman wiped his moist lips
With a tattered handkerchief.

Presently the butcher said:
"Judge, here's a good feed for that dog."
The old gentleman took the package and thanked him,
And the courtly bow he gave was a survival
Of a bygone age of Virginian chivalry.

With his hairy arms folded,
The butcher leaned upon the shining showcase
And watched the departing figure
Enter the wintry street.

Nottley the Embalmer

A man in my business
Discovers things
That even the doctors and the police
Don't know about.

If you've lived in Harlem,
You've doubtless heard about old Mr. Weaver.
Perhaps you've seen him
Strolling along Manhattan Avenue in the morning.
He did that for years.

My grandmother says
That when she was just a girl
He was a realtor in Harlem,
And he was just as peculiar then
As he ever was.

He never went to church.
He never had a male friend.
He never was seen with a woman.
He was like a tree standing by itself on the prairie.

He wore the same clothes for years,
And he never seemed to wear them out.
People wondered and wondered,
And they are still wondering about Mr. Weaver.

When I embalmed him,
I found out what Sister Cripens would give a fortune to know:
I discovered that Mr. Weaver was a eunuch.

Mrs. Marcella Loften

Mrs. Marcella Loften was a good Christian woman
And a great lover of little children . . .
Anybody in the neighborhood would tell you that.
The dear lady observed on numberless occasions:
"My greatest tragedy
Is that I have no little ones of my own."

When Mrs. Marcella Loften said this,
She always left hearers with the impression
That the fault was not hers
But her husband's.

She thereby gained maximal sympathy
From virtuous wives who inferred
That the wild oats Mr. Loften had sown
In his unhallowed youth
Had left him wanting in his marital state.

The children were very fond of Mrs. Loften,
For she told them dramatic fables and parables
And made for them delicious cookies and candies.

Thus Mrs. Marcella Loften was able to secure
From the most bashful and reticent little boys and girls
The intimate secrets of their parents.

Richard Birch

Richard's mother was a music teacher
And her overweening ambition
Was to make her son a celebrated pianist.
She believed that a child could be bent,
Like a twig . . . in any direction.
So Richard's lessons began
When he was just large enough to sit at a piano.

Through the slow-moving years
She compelled him to practice long and hard.
He learned to read notes with amazing rapidity
And to finger the most intricate compositions.

He appeared in piano recitals
At some of the larger churches in Harlem;
And the audiences, unmoved,
Sat watching his calculating gestures
As one follows curiously the actions of an expert mechanic.

He attended the best recitals in Carnegie Hall,
And his mother bought him expensive music journals
And the biographies of great composers,
Hoping thereby to inspire him.
Later she made cruel sacrifices
To put him through a famous conservatory;
But as the unpitying years passed
His efforts and her efforts came to naught.

Then she heard about a famous Russian teacher
Who had recently established a studio in Brooklyn,
And she hastened to him with Richard. . . .

Mrs. Birch let two endless weeks crawl by
Before she called again to question the great man
Concerning her son's ability.

The master frowned,
Wove his long fingers through his massive beard,
Cleared his throat and said:

"Madam, your son's soul is wooden.
Verve . . . the divine spark . . . is lacking utterly.
If I taught him—if a Paderewski taught him—a hundred years,
Richard Birch would still be what he is.
A mechanical manipulator of piano keys."

Aunt Hagar

De world is gittin' bad an' badder
Because de preachers has done forgot how to preach.
A purson kin go to church nowadays,
Year in an' year out,
An' never hear a sermon dat reaches de heart.

Take dat young preacher we got at Mount Gilead.
He's been to all dem big colleges,
An' he's got three or four big degrees,
An' he ain't never learned how to preach.
He jest stands up there in de pulpit
Peerin' over his glasses,
Like he's tryin' to find de words on his paper,
His voice dronin' like a sick bee's.

I always said dat preachin' couldn't be taught.
Now I knows it. Yes, Lawd, I knows it!
When Gawd calls a man to preach,
Gawd gives him his sermons;
An' he don't have to look through a whole lot ov books
To find somethin' to say.

I like to see a preacher open his mouth
An' let Gawd fill it with de bread ov life.
I like to see a man throw his head back an' holler
An' set de church on fire with de Gospel.
I like to see a preacher walk up an' down de pulpit,
Talkin' with de Master.

How kin a man expect to persuade other folks
When he ain't persuaded hisself?
How kin a man expect de congregation to remember somethin'
Dat he cain't remember hisself?

People don't go to church to hear no lecture.
Dey go to hear preachin'.
Jesus didn't git up in de synagogue
Readin' off no paper.
De world is gittin' bad an' badder
Because de preachers has done forgot how to preach.

Little Nellie Patmore

She was proud of the mysterious woman
Who was her mother,
The woman whose dusky loveliness
Snared backward glances in the street.

She loved the mysterious woman
Whose moods were variable as a weathercock.
The child was equally puzzled when her mother
Withdrew into an oasis of silence
Or vivified the sumptuous rooms with sudden gaieties.

The years went by
Like slow-motion figures in a pantomime,
And Little Nellie Patmore's mother
Became more taciturn and sad-voiced.

Life penciled its mystery
On the loveliness of her face
And touched
The dusk of her hair with gray.

One afternoon
Little Nellie Patmore had a quarrel
With her playmate across the corridor,
And her small neighbor
Blew out the light of the sun
With a single breath:
"I wouldn't have a mother kept by a white man!"

Mother Vibbard

Twenty-five presidents have come and gone
Since Mother Vibbard first saw the light of day
In a tumble-down shack near Richmond, Virginia.

Hair as white as cotton,
Eyes as clear as a crystal glass
Face as impassive as a Stoic's,
Hollow shoulders covered with a thick woolen shawl
Held together by an enormous brass safety pin . . .
Mother Vibbard sits in her rocking chair reading her Bible.

Mother Vibbard remembers Abraham Lincoln
Walking through the streets of Richmond,
Holding his son Tad by the hand.

Mother Vibbard remembers black slaves
Prostrating themselves at his feet,
While from a great height came a sad, sad voice:
"You must kneel to God only.
I am but God's humble instrument;
But you may rest assured that as long as I live
No one shall put a shackle on your limbs."

Mother Vibbard remembers the old slave
Who whispered, awe-stricken, that he lifted his hat
And President Lincoln lifted his!

Twenty-five presidents have come and gone . . .
And Mother Vibbard sits in her rocking chair reading her Bible.

Miss Emile Housman

Miss Emile Housman was white and thirty-eight.
She had lived as a girl in Macon, Georgia,
And her years in New York had not changed
The impressions of her adolescence.
Miss Emile graduated with Negroes from the university,
But she still believed,
With that great biblical scholar, Dr. Charles Carroll,
That God is white and the Negro a beast
Created to serve his white master.

Sometimes Miss Emile Housman came across
The achievements of Negroes in books and magazines and newspapers.
The lady pointed to these as exceptions,
And still believed that black folk
Are lazy, unmoral, criminal, irresponsible, religious,
Sensual, childish, filthy, and unintellectual;
And Miss Emile Housman was careful to read books
That sustained the ideas picked up in Macon, Georgia.

The lady was a firm believer
In the Fatherhood of God and the Brotherhood of Man.
She taught in both a public school and a Sunday school.
She always secured a transfer for herself or the Negro pupil
If one appeared in her classroom;
Miss Emile Housman did not believe in giving sanction
To any form of social equality.
She would sigh in the presence of her colleagues:
"You Northerners are so ignorant of niggers."

The Honorable Eutaw Lamb

The Honorable Eutaw Lamb died of heart disease
In his law office on One Hundred and Thirty-fifth Street.
He was a well-known figure
In the civic, fraternal, political, and religious life of Harlem.
Six months before he died,
He gave old Judge Crimpton this will:

To my wife I leave her love of Big Shot Lacy.
Hereafter, when she visits their love nest in that apartment house
Across the street from the YWCA,
She won't have to lie about going to the Harlem Uplifters' Club.

To my mother-in-law I leave a vacuum.
Her nagging tongue and self-advertised goodness
Hurried me to my grave.

To my pastor, the Reverend Hart Newman,
I leave five hundred dollars.
The Sabbath is a day of rest.
And many a Sunday morning
The soothing voice of the Reverend Hart Newman
Lulled me to sleep in the Shiloh Baptist Church.

To my son I leave the pleasure of making a living.
For thirty long years
He thought the pleasure was mine.

To my daughter I leave one thousand dollars.
This will enable her to spend the summer in Atlantic City
With her sweet man, Diamond Canady.

To my cook I leave all the food and all the scandals
She carried out of my kitchen
During the last ten years.

To Ma Goodwin I leave my Sugar Hill apartments . . .
When I was homeless,
She took me in;
When I was hungry,
She fed me.

176

Simon Southorn

On the last page of Mr. Masters's novel,
The Soul of Simon Southorn,
The hero dies a lingering death.
Mr. Masters would have rendered a great service
To Simon, to the reader, and to literature,
If he had let his hero die
Three hundred pages earlier.

Mr. Masters did not make his purpose clear
In the one-hundred-thousand words of his *magnum opus*;
But the brilliant writer has three chances left,
Since this is the initial volume of a tetralogy.

Simon, the hero, was born in Okay, Arkansas,
With a veil over his eyes.
In a rare moment of lucidity
Mr. Masters says on page one:
"A baby born with a veil over its face can see things."
Nevertheless Simon blunders through the remaining
Two hundred and ninety-nine pages.

Mr. Masters has been called
The most subtle writer in the Harlem Renaissance.
A famous man is an Atlas.
To support his reputation,
Mr. Masters becomes so subtle
There is no danger of anyone's detecting his meaning.

His novel is a no-man's-land
Of mutilated experiences.
His diction consists of crutches
On which the characters hobble
From sentence to sentence.
His style is that of a meat cleaver
Finishing tainted dog scraps.
That he believes in capital punishment
His sincerest supporters cannot doubt,
For he hangs phrases and clauses on every page.

Through a topsyturvydom of episodes,
Simon wanders to find his soul.
He is plagued with sex
Like a bitch in heat.
Mr. Masters tries to rid his hero
Of this obsession
By leading him through sexual bouts
With durable cottonfield wenches
And Beale Street whores.

At intervals Mr. Masters pauses
To weep over the plight of Simon,
But I do not blame him for this.

Reading
The Soul of Simon Southorn
Is like going over Niagara Falls in a barrel.

Aunt Martha

The gloomy doorway of the apartment house
Framed the specter-figure of the aged woman
Who stood there shivering, a frayed rusty black cape
Drawn tightly about her fleshless shoulders.

Her eyes fixed on the pieces of battered furniture
In a dreary huddle on the cold pavement,
She thought of the one-dollar bill
Crumpled in the top of her cotton stocking.

She shuffled into the dilapidated hallway
And told the drowsy elevator boy to watch her things
While she went to the little mission around the corner.

Sitting in front of the shabby altar,
Aunt Martha sang and prayed and forgot her troubles.
When the Reverend Joshua Lovelace
Announced hymn number 11,
And a bustling deacon raised the collection,
Aunt Martha placed ten cents on the ancient walnut table
And repeated the mystical number again and again.

That night, feeling strangely happy,
She sat in the dim vestibule
Dozing at intervals and watching her precious furniture.

The next morning she gave the figures 711,
With unwonted stealth and a guilty conscience,
To a Numbers agent named Jazz Boker,
Who, surprised, took the ninety cents,
Gave the old woman a pink slip in exchange,
And played the money on the 711 combination. . . .

While arranging her pieces of battered furniture
In her new quarters, late that evening,
Aunt Martha sang triumphantly:
Gawd moves in a mysterious way,
His wondahs to perform. . . .

Ivory Frysinger

Though he drank nothing stronger than black coffee
And avoided love affairs with easy women
And never gambled,
Ivory was a welcome guest in shady resorts.
Proprietors were glad to see his moony grin
Because he attracted wandering customers.

Okay Katie said
That liquor and gambling and a double-dealing woman
Had made him what he was:
An itinerant piano player
Who sang in a plaintive baritone
And wrung from the ivory keys
Astonishing rhythms.

Sometimes a hollow-eyed black Ulysses would say:
"I'm homesick, Ivory, homesick,
Strike up Papa Handy's 'St. Louis Blues' "

Sometimes a hard-faced woman
Would whisper in his ear
As he sat hunched over a battered piano:
"Ivory, last night bad luck overtook me.
Let a good woman hear them 'Loveless Blues.' "

Since playing and singing for the benefit of others
Was Ivory's religion,
No one had ever heard him refuse to grant a request.

When Ivory played
His mind became a tapestry of color-tones.
With his head sidewise
As if taking a cue
From someone hidden in the sanctum of the piano,
His sensitive fingers caressed the ivories,
His full-bodied baritone swam into the verse,
His ebony face glowed with wonder.
When Ivory sang
Folk forgot to talk.

Sometimes his winging fingers
Dipped lightly over the keys
Like the shadows of gulls
Skimming the surface of mirroring waters.

180

Sometimes his rigid fingers fell
Like pneumatic hammers
Upon the quaking keyboard.

Ivory's mad genius
Could change the shape and the mood of music
By fashioning an anthem into a waltz,
Or a spiritual into blues,
Or a classic into jazz.

Alexander Calverton

Mr. Alexander Calverton,
President of the Harlem Savings Bank,
Chairman of the Deacon Board at Mt. Sinai,
Boasted that he was a self-made man.

He told the lowly that what he had done
Any other member of his race could do
If he had the stuff in him
And put his hand in God's hand.

I got shoes, you got shoes,
All Gawd's chillun got shoes.

Mr. Calverton stood on Sunday at the collection table,
A blazing diamond on the bosom of his immaculate shirt—
A self-made man and good Christian whom God had prospered.

Mr. Calverton had forgot his old black mammy
In that shack on the Red River—
The old black mammy who had slipped food at night
Out of the white folks' kitchen to feed her son.

Mr. Calverton had forgot old Sister Carrie,
Who had taken him in one wintry night
When she had seen him wandering in a deserted entranceway,
Crazed with cold and hunger.

Mr. Calverton had forgot
The thousands of poor black folk
Who had put the savings of a lifetime into his bank.

181

Silent Sam

Etta and Silent Sam couldn't marry
Because his wife, Emily,
refused to divorce him.

Ignoring her mother's pleas
And her friends' protests
And her own pride,
Etta went to live with Silent Sam
As his common-law wife.

Nine years later
Sister Cripens brought the news
That Emily had died Easter morning
In the arms of Jesus.

Etta hurried to Mr. Caruso's market
On Eighth Avenue,
And bought two huge baskets of groceries:
She and Silent Sam would celebrate
With a big dinner,
And then go to the Harlem Opera House
To see the little brown-skinned comedienne
Admired by the Prince of Wales.

The dinner hour passed,
But Silent Sam didn't come home.
The food dried up on the gas stove
As she sat up that night
Waiting for him.

On her way to the police station
She took a letter
From the mailbox in the hallway,
Opened it with frantic fingers, and read:

"Dear Etta:
I know this will hurt you bad,
For it's almost killing me.
Emily sent for me just before she died
And made me promise
I'd never have anything to do with you
Any more.

Emily said if I didn't make this vow
On my bended knees before God
She would go to hell hating me
And her ghost would come back
To torment me all my days.

"I made the promise
And Emily died smiling and blessing the Lord.
You can have all the things in the house,
Because I'm traveling West today;
But remember that your loving Sam
Will love you forever."

Duke Huggins

Duke Huggins was master of the Subway,
A gambling den housed in the sheltering shadows
Of a chambered basement on Upper Lenox Avenue.

He was a bronze colossus of a man
With restless gray eyes
Whose hollow chest was framed by enormous shoulders
Bowed from sitting hunched over gaming tables
Through long, tightening hours.

His mobile fingers
Were as sensitive to the touch of cards
As those of a Paderewski to the keys of a piano.
With a glance he could measure a man,
And he knew how to deal with his man
To get what he wanted.

He changed his clothes three times a day
And was called the best-dressed man in Harlem.
Karl Krafft, the little Jewish tailor,
Held him up as a model
For other Harlem sports and would-be sports.

The gambling fraternity frequented two spacious rooms
Containing pool tables for shooting craps
And card tables for poker, casino, Georgia skin, and blackjack.
Chauffeurs, janitors, bellhops, porters, students,
Waiters, cooks, taxicab drivers, clerks,
Dope peddlers, and sweet men haunted the Subway,
While loose-lipped derelicts with greedy eyes
Watched for a chance to beg a drink
From the arrogant winners.

Green shades shaped the cones of light
Upon the padded tables, revealing the faces of players
Who masked or tried to mask their fluxing emotions.

184

Like fragments of fog, jagged smoke-clouds
Drifted upward from cigarettes and cigars;
And about the tables stood sharp-eyed gazers
Learning the art of hazard from unholy masters
Whose curses and impious epithets
Beat against the daubed walls
Like breakers wasting themselves on a desolate shore.

Big Blue, the Titanesque house man,
Moved, catlike, from table to table.
Duke Huggins, quiet, speculative,
A fat cigar clamped between his ivory teeth,
His black derby perched perilously
On the back of his head,
Sat upon an iron-and-steel safe in a far corner
Fingering his diamond-studded watch.

Reverend Isaiah Cloud

The Reverend Isaiah Cloud preached a doctrine
That wormed its way under the skins of churchgoers.
Like an expert sharpshooter,
He hit tirelessly the bull's-eye of their egotisms.

He never preached in pleasing generalities,
But discoursed on specific private sins and social corruptions
That left no hearer with that lofty hypocrisy:
"I thank God that I am not like other men!"

Instead of mouthing the hollow words,
The Brotherhood of Man and the Fatherhood of God,
He leveled the social barriers in the church
And practiced a simple democracy.
Napoleon Hannibal Speare and Grand Chancellor Sackville
Received no more consideration
Than poor Sister Carrie and Aunt Hilda.

Continual self-analysis had taught him
The weakness of other folk
And ironed out the frailties in his own individuality.

When the depression came,
He let beggars and tramps sleep in the church,
And he had the Sisters of Charity serve them.
Society matrons found themselves doing
For the beggars and tramps of Harlem
What they had never done for themselves and their husbands.
The Harlem Advocate carried the headline:
"Aristocratic Church Becomes Communistic!"

You marveled how the little man
Could tell you so much about yourself.
Probing your motives and conduct
And revealing the cancerous and unseemly,
He made you feel naked and ashamed.

The challenge was always there . . .
In his eye, in his voice, in his manner.
It stung you, grilled you, haunted you.
The challenge seemed to say:
"He who is without sin let him cast the first stone!"

186

Surprise, chagrin, consternation . . .
Then anger and conspiracy came
Into the house of God.

Finding naught of reproach in the man's character,
Napoleon Hannibal Speare and Knapp Sackville,
Voicing . . . as they said . . .
The opinion of the membership,
Declared he was a preacher and not a pastor:
The debt on the church proved that . . .
So they let him go!

Ezra Crane

Ezra went to a training camp
With the draftees from Carthage, Mississippi—
Patriotic blacks sent to the army
By patriotic whites
Who served their country at home.

Ezra enjoyed his trip to France,
Received a Croix de Guerre
For killing on outpost duty
Five scared Germans who scared him,
And returned to his hometown a hero.

The black citizens received Corporal Crane
In the Bedrock Baptist Church,
With flaring oratory and tempestuous applause,
And excited mothers held up their jet-eyed babes
To get a glimpse of him.

The following day
Corporal Crane walked into Mr. Horne's general store
To buy a package of cigarettes,
And forgot to take off his hat.
Mr. Horne, insulted,
Swore that the nigger didn't know his place
Because those crazy Frenchmen
Had put notions of social equality into his head.

Despite his anger,
Mr. Horne saw clearly the momentous issues involved
When the uppity nigger
Got out of his place,
And he was mindful of a white man's duty in Mississippi.

And thus it happened that old Mr. Horne,
While attempting to kick Ezra out of his store,
Slipped and broke his leg.

Ezra is now safe in Harlem,
Having escaped that night on a freight train,
Unknown to the white citizens gunning for
That big burly nigger soldier
Who attacked old Mr. Horne.

Big Jim Casey

Big Jim Casey,
Jailbird,
Friend of the Workers,
Agitator for a New Republic . . . .
Big Jim Casey,
Whose voice could roar like thunders
Leaping from crag to crag,
Or grow as tender as a mammy's lullaby—
Big Jim Casey was shot through the lung last week
By a militiaman in a Colorado strike,
And tonight his comrades will have his funeral
In Liberty Hall.

During a Mississippi flood,
Big Jim Casey escaped from Major Hardy's plantation,
Where three generations of Caseys had worked
Without being able to get out of the Major's debt.

Hearing Eugene Debs
Talk to some workingmen in Chicago,
Big Jim Casey saw a vision hidden from the many.

With his idol surrounded on the platform
By the somber faces of men with insensible hands,
Big Jim Casey said:
"Here, now, is Eugene Debs, defender ov common folks . . .
A man the latches ov whose shoes
I ain't worthy to unlace."

Talking to black strikebreakers in Pittsburgh,
Big Jim Casey said:
"The white workers an' black workers must git together.
Cain't you see, ma friends,
The big bosses is playin'
The whites an' blacks agin each other?"

Big Jim Casey,
Black as the Delta mud,
Strong as a Delta mule,
Patient as a Delta ox . . .
Towering and awkward,
With the sadness of wisdom in his face . . .
Big Jim Casey . . .
The quaintness of his humor made you laugh,
The common sense of his arguments stuck in your mind,
The rhythm of his eloquence matched the rhythm of your blood.

Big Jim Casey,
Jailbird,
Friend of the Workers,
Agitator for a New Republic . . .
Big Jim Casey,
Coughing up blood in a dimly lighted shack,
Dying while the hard-muscled arm of a white miner
Supported his tremendous black shoulders—
Big Jim Casey pushed back the shadows
Trooping into his mind to say:
"The white an' black workers must . . . git . . . together."

Freida Maynard

That afternoon Adolphus told Freida
He had to go to Brooklyn on business;
So he'd be unable to attend the Charity Ball.

Since their engagement,
They'd always gone to such affairs together;
And Freida, being disappointed and a little restless,
Decided to see Cab Calloway at the LaFayette.
But while walking down St. Nicholas Avenue,
She met the Paul Benefields
And they persuaded her to go to the Rockland Palace.

The jungle rhythms of the Duke's jazz band,
The thrill of dancers executing colorful patterns,
The liveliness of old friends,
And the novelty of new acquaintances—
These lifted Freida out of the bog of disappointment.

Freida stood near the dance floor,
Laughing at a new joke Paul Benefield had heard
At the Harlem Opera House,
When she glimpsed Adolphus dancing past
With the notorious Ginger Barry from The Club Alabam.

"Excuse me, Paul," said Freida,
Leaving him abruptly.
Paul scratched his head foolishly as she faded into the crowd,
He shrugged his shoulders. "Now, ain't that something?"

"You dance like an angel," Adolphus told the glamorous Ginger.
She looked up at him from under long, black lashes,
The curves of her body following him through intricate rhythms.
"You're not so bad yourself," she rollicked.
He drew her closer. . . .

The heel of a woman's shoe thudded on the man's skull.
Surprised and pained, Adolphus groaned:
"My God, Freida!"
As he backed away,
She pursued him like a relentless little fury,
Whacking him with the heel of her shoe.
"Give 'im hell, Sister!" exclaimed a plum-colored woman.
The onlookers guffawed.
Ginger Barry from The Club Alabam
Walked away disdainfully,
Her plump hips swaying to the rhythms of "Stormy Weather."

191

Xavier van Loon

The plague had ravaged the plains of North Dakota.
He stood in the desolate field,
The scorching wind in his nostrils,
The stripped earth under his feet,
The torch of the sun in his face.
He staggered across the black pasture . . .
Staggered, unseeing, past the starved mare
That half-raised her head, whinnied, and grew stiff.

He traveled East on the rods,
Stopping now and then to preach and sing in small churches,
Thrilling the people with his dramatic powers.

Seeing Charles Gilpin at the Provincetown Playhouse
In *The Emperor Jones*,
He decided to become an actor.

The great Ziegfeld heard him in *Rang Tang*
And gave him the part of Joe in *Show Boat*,
The role that brought him fame and fortune.
London and Paris and Berlin have honored his genius,
And Hollywood has borrowed him from the stage.

A European critic said
That one night at the Savoy Theatre
He saw in the black actor's face
The tragedy of aboriginal man
Trapped in a desolation.

Marzimmu Heffner

The headline of *The Harlem Advocate* exclaimed:
"Only Living African Slave Is in Harlem!"

He came from the Coromantees of the Gold Coast;
And, in spite of the drubbings of time and circumstance,
He retains something of the Spartan hardiness and fortitude
That signalized his proud forebears.

He was a boy when his native village was burned in the night.
Five slave-raiders overpowered his father, the chief.
Tortured by the disgrace,
His sire attempted suicide.

"We are not Whydahs, nor Nagoes, nor Pawpaws!" he said.
"We Coromantees are men . . . free . . . men!"

He remembers the infernal journey to the coast;
The ravages of jungle and flood, of famine and beast;
The polluting breaths of swamps and the chilling poisons of uplands;
The vultures that shadowed the coffles.

He remembers the horrors of the middle passage;
The victims packed between decks like sardines in a can;
The vertical brassy sun and the shortage of food and water;
The stench and seasickness, the brutalities and prayers.

Then came the epidemic of smallpox.
The captain ordered the diseased slaves to be thrown overboard
And the others brought upon deck, unshackled.
Some were assigned work with the diminished crew.

While his father was planning a mutiny,
He was apprehended and hanged from a mast.
For months and months
The slaver wormed its way through the rotting seas,
Evading armed vessels on police duty.
Finally it reached a secret port
On the Gulf of Mexico.

Months later, Marzimmu's serpentine trail
Reached a vast plantation in Florida. . . .
One stormy night he ran off to the Everglades,
Where he was taken in by the Seminoles.
When the first gun was fired at Fort Sumter,
He did not know a score of English words. . . .

The unresting blood of the Coromantees
Made him a wanderer in many lands:
He has worked on docks in Shanghai and Capetown,
In Marseilles and London, in New Orleans and San Francisco;
He has been a stoker on tramps in the Caribbean Sea;
He has worked on plantations in Cuba and Central America.
With the sun of his life slanting low in the West,
He came to Harlem to die.

Marzimmu is now a celebrity.
Metropolitan papers carry his picture.
He is happy . . . at last . . . in the land of his servitude.

Gladys Zimmerman

Out in Tucson, Arizona,
The night the guests gathered for her marriage to John Levine,
Gladys Zimmerman, suitcase in hand,
Climbed into the Ford of Pretty Boy Bitts
And started for Harlem.

They rested and sported a day or two
In El Paso, Little Rock, St. Louis, Chicago, and Pittsburgh.
Gladys wrote her heartburning widowed mother in each city,
Describing her love for Pretty Boy Bitts
And the way he was spending money on her.

In every letter Mrs. Zimmerman told Gladys
How well John Levine was doing in his tailor business
And that he still wanted to marry her.

Two years later in Harlem
Pretty Boy Bitts grew tired of Gladys
And became the common-law husband of a Spanish dancer
Living on One Hundred and Fourteenth Street.
Gladys wrote her mother she was the secretary
To a prominent real estate dealer.

One evening John Levine's cousin, Ramblin' Hicks,
Was strolling down Lenox Avenue
When a hard-eyed streetwalker tempted him.
Too late, Gladys recognized the man from her hometown.
Ramblin' Hicks returned to Tucson and told John Levine
It was a good thing he hadn't got a whore for a wife.
The next morning the body of John Levine was found
Hanging by the neck from an iron pipe in his tailor shop.

Freemon Hawthorne

When I was a boy in the Ozarks
I used to go into grandfather's barn
To watch old Caesar match his feline cunning
With the cunning of the rats.

One summer there was a drought,
And the rats became desperate with hunger
And withered shadows of themselves.

My grandfather said:
"Keep old Caesar out of the barn . . .
For a hungry rat is a sensible rat."

But when I crawled into my trundle bed at night
Old Caesar would sneak down to the barn.

One morning I found his remains
In a dark corner,
His bones clean . . . clean as a toothpick.

Coming through the park today,
I saw in the eyes of hungry men
The same look of desperation
That I used to see
In the eyes of the rats
In my grandfather's barn
In the Ozarks.

196

Laughing Jim

I was borned wid laughtah in ma heaht, O Lawd,
Gonna die wid a grin on ma face!

How Laughing Jim could laugh!
Gales of jollity from the region below his belt
Rushed upward through the cavern of his mouth,
And the whites of his eyes and his pearly teeth
Gleamed like crystal snowflakes on patches of dark grass
In the black mud of the Yazoo Bottoms.

Once Laughing Jim's ma threw a skillet at him
For stealing a watermelon from old Eyetalian Joe,
The Lenox Avenue huckster;
Later, when Jim saw her eyes shining
As her greedy fingers stroked the melon,
Jim laughed.

Once the great revivalist, Samson Doolittle, declared
That hell was full of gin and blues and good-looking whores.
Jim laughed,
And a pompous deacon put him out of the church.

I was borned wid laughtah in ma heaht, O Lawd,
Gonna die wid a grin on ma face!

One Saturday night
Laughing Jim's wife ran off
with Big Boy Casey,
The policy agent living next door;
And a week later
Laughing Jim discovered the lovers
Coming out of a cheap rooming house
On Manhattan Avenue. . . .

When the giant Irish policeman
Stepped over the bullet-riddled bodies
And took the warm thirty-eight
From Jim's cold fingers,
Jim laughed.

I was borned wid laughtah in ma heaht, O Lawd,
Gonna die wid a grin on ma face.

197

Goldie Keats

The dusk of her luxuriant hair
Frames the golden-brown loveliness of her face.
The blue-black pools of her eyes
Mirror a subtle invitation,
And the utter allure of her fresh red lips
Begs for a bruising kiss.

I have seen the poetry of motion:
A sleek tiger form
Gliding through light and shadow,
Its flexing muscles rhythmical with beauty;
Goldie's exquisite body
Passing in the street . . .
The healthy blossoms of her bosom
And the clean curves of her hips
And the lyrical sturdiness of her legs
Charming passers-by.

A hundred men have dreamed of making love to her
While making love to others.
Two score and ten good husbands
Would leave their wives for her,
And a dozen lovers would die for her.
But Goldie is a luscious fruit
Hanging just beyond a hungry man's reach.

Hilmar Enick

The odyssey is ended:
He has discovered a land where the tragedy of color
Is a dimly remembered dream.

He writes from Moscow
In the former salon of Princess Shakhovaskaya,
Where the babel of conquering proletarians—
German, Russian, Spanish, Chinese, and English—
Swirls along the elegant staircase
Of a bygone dynasty.

On the Dark Continent
Of his fathers' fathers
He was an alien.
In the caste-bitter land of his nativity
He was a pariah.
In the Orient
He was a prank that kismet played
In an idle moment.

Now he is a man, an equal, a comrade
Of the Club of Foreign Workers
Building a new civilization
With Brotherhood as the cornerstone.

His odyssey is ended:
He has discovered a land where the tragedy of color
Is a dimly remembered dream.

Uncle Twitty

Uncle Twitty encountered the little Puerto Rican
In an Australian's saloon, twenty-three years ago.

Their friendship throve like cottonseed
Planted in the black soil of the Sabine Valley.

Together they saw the prodding years
Cross barren flats and climb gutted crags.

Together they saw their sons go to war
With eyes ashine and hopes upleaping.

The young Puerto Rican returned from no-man's-land,
Broken in spirit, with decay in his lungs.

The black American's son came back to a bootlegger's dive,
Despoiled of illusions, with revolt in his heart.

The two friends, over their bottle of bootleg gin,
Worry with the how and the why of human existence.

Uncle Twitty thinks things are bad
Because people fail to obey the Ten Commandments.

The little Puerto Rican argues that the profit motive
Produced the tragedy of man and the tyranny of things.

The Puerto Rican takes his troubles to Uncle Twitty,
And Uncle Twitty carries his to the Good Will Baptist Church.

Bella Scarritt

The Benchleys had gone to Philadelphia
To visit Mrs. Benchley's invalid mother.

Bella, left alone in the apartment,
Gave a party for her Harlem friends,
Cooking a big chicken dinner
And serving fine liquors
From Mr. Benchley's imported stock.

The Harlemites made themselves at home,
Lounging in the elegant chairs,
Playing the grand radio,
Doing the Black Bottom and Lindy Hop and Slow Drag,
Smoking Mr. Benchley's gold-tipped cigarettes.

A blue-black woman teased her urgent lover
With the rhythms of her undulating body
And sang in a lush voice:

When the cat's away,
The mice will play.
When the white folks take a trip,
Po' niggers have their day.

A frail yellow man of middle age
Who owned a small restaurant on Lenox Avenue
Was arguing with a red-headed girl
Perched on the arm of his chair.

"The young nigger ain't no good," said the yellow man;
"He's got a beer pocketbook an' a champagne mind."
The red-headed girl fell across his knees, giggling.

Bella lay on a divan
In the arms of her nut-brown daddy
From Jersey City.

"If I had you an' a house like this,"
She said,
"I'd be in paradise.
Jimmie, why is it white folks git all the good things in life
An' we niggers have to steal our sweets?"

The front door opened into the hall.
The blue-black woman cried:
"My Gawd, here comes the white folks!"

The Harlemites,
Grabbing wine glasses and littered plates
Fled toward the kitchen,
Like mice at the approach of a house cat.

Mr. and Mrs. Benchley came into the upset parlor,
Catching glimpses of the hurrying figures.
Mr. Benchley's gray eyes glittered.
He sank upon a chair and guffawed.
Mrs. Benchley's classic features grew severe.
"You might control yourself, Bob," she suggested icily.

Edna Borland

"Ma . . . ma!" the baby voices wailed. "Ma . . .ma!"
The twins lay side by side
On the shreddy quilt flung across the bed.
Their skinny black hands and feet
Thrashed the soiled air,
And their round eyes, like jet beads, glistened with tears.

An emptied, bluish-gray milk bottle,
With a torn, ashy-black nipple,
Had wormed itself under a greasy pillow.
"Ma . . . ma! . . . Ma . . . ma!"
There was an urgency born of hunger
In their voices;
An anonymous fear haunted their oldish baby faces.

The mother stood at the open window,
Looking down into Lenox Avenue.
On an enfeebled table braced by a pine box,
A decrepit radio conjured the topsy-turvy flat
With flickering blues rhythms,
And then a sepulchral contralto sobbed a grievance:

What can I do when everything goes wrong?
What can I do when everything goes wrong?
Ain't no more good since ma sweet man is gone.

The mother suddenly lifted her arms
In a gesture of supplication,
And from her swollen throat
Came an unearthly crescendo of madness,
And the hot tears dribbled into the furrows of agony
That puckered the black face. . . .

A man crossing Lenox Avenue
Glanced up and remained like a statue,
As the fantasy of a woman flashed through space. . . .

"Ma . . . ma!" the baby voices wailed: "Ma . . . ma!"
And from the battered radio came the contralto's dark lament:
Ain't no more good since ma sweet man is gone.

Slick Gunnar

Upper Lenox was gay with colored lights and colored people
Forming a panorama of kaleidoscopic patterns.

As Slick Gunnar came out of Tony the Greek's poolroom,
A dozen shots ripped through the avenue's medley of sounds.

The chief of the federal agents, his ugly gat smoking,
Approached the writhing outlaw, with a cold half-smile.

An old black woman was among the curious crowd.
Seeing the dead-white face, she moaned: "O Jesus!"

A few minutes later a siren sounded and the crowd parted.
The dying outlaw was shoved into the ambulance.

The onlookers heard the chief of the federal agents say:
"That's the end of Slick Gunnar, Public Enemy Number One."

The government men were a little puzzled to see pity
Flowing into the black and yellow and brown faces.

A pasty-faced man remarked, with a tight grin:
"He got what was comin' to 'im; he's bad as they make 'em."

The old black woman looked up at the pasty-faced man.
She was thinking of her son who was to die in Sing Sing.

Her voice cracked with anger and sorrow:
"You says dat po' fellah is bad, Mistah? What made 'im bad?"

A hush enveloped the crowd . . . a profound hush.
The pasty-faced man grinned foolishly . . . and turned away.

Frank Fullilove

Frank Fullilove was the editor of *The Black Masses*.
He had been a reporter on *The Negro World*,
The mouthpiece of the imperial Marcus Garvey's
Back-to-Africa movement;
But with the Icarian fall of his hero,
Frank Fullilove joined the Socialists.

In his dingy little office on Upper Seventh Avenue,
He wrote his fiery editorials
To the black masses of America.

Sometimes he delivered speeches
In his precise Oxford English,
And in the open forum he could parry and thrust
With the ablest dialecticians.
He secretly scorned
His poor white comrades who knew nothing
About history and economics and sociology,
And who mangled the beautiful English language
Of which he was inordinately proud.

He possessed the West Indian's hatred
Of the docility in American blacks;
Yet he admired the dusky beauty of their women.
He thought the South a hellhole
And was suspicious of every white Southern comrade.
He had said a thousand times in *The Black Masses*:
"The Socialist party is the ship; all else . . . the sea!"

Nana Swancy

They were sitting on the sofa
In the rose-tinted light of the floor lamp
When Blake asked her to marry him.
Nana winced. Should she tell him all?
Tragic memories drugged her senses . . . .

The ugly courtroom at Thebes, Alabama,
The first floor crowded with giggling whites;
The dirty gallery, with twittering Negroes.
Nana's mother had had Tipsy Goins arrested.
Judge White was hard on rascals
Who got women in a family way and didn't marry them.
Everybody in Gallatin County knew that.
Then, too, Nana's mother worked for the Judge.

His Honor was good and sore.
Hadn't the stubborn nigger said he'd go to jail
Because the child wasn't his?
"Whose is it?" Judge White demanded.
Tipsy Goins dropped his head.
"Answer me, nigger!" shouted Judge White. "Whose is it?"
Nana leaped to her feet. "Your son's!" she screamed. . . .

As they sat on the sofa,
Tragic memories drugged Nana's senses.
Should she tell him all?
"Blake," said Nana, "marriage is a serious thing,
Please give me more time to think it over."

Uncle Lash

For the last fifty years I been hearin'
Black folks talkin' 'bout buildin' up race business—
When I was in Waycross, Georgia,
An' on Eighteenth Street in Kansas City
An' on Texas Avenue in Shreveport
An' on Thirty-fifth Street in Chicago.

Here in Harlem,
Editor Napoleon Hannibal Speare
Is always writin' in the *Advocate*,
An' Banker Alexander Calverton
Is always talkin' in church,
An' Grand Chancellor Knapp Sackville
Is always lecturin' to us poor folks in lodge meetin's,
An' Brother Hester is always argerfyin' in the grocery store—
All them big Negroes is always tellin' us poor folks
That the trouble with the race
Is that we ain't got no race pride
An' we don't support Negro business.

Pursonally, I got plenty of race pride,
But I tell you I git sick an' tired
A-hearin' big folks talk 'bout Negro business.

If I goes to Brother Hester's
An' buys twenty-five cents' worth of sugar,
He gives me fifteen cents' worth of sugar,
An' ten cents' worth of color an' race pride.

After fifty years of seein' things an' thinkin',
I ain't so sure 'bout this savin' the race
By buildin' up Negro business.
My old woman is sure it will,
But I been tellin' her
That business lives on them that buys
An' makes money fer them that sells.

I been sayin' to my old woman again an' again,
If buildin' up Negro business
Will help the race as much as
Editor Napoleon Hannibal Speare
An' Banker Alexander Calverton
An' Grand Chancellor Knapp Sackville
An' Groceryman Brother Hester
Says it will help the race—
Then why is it I sees so many poor white folks
With nothin' to eat an' nowhere to stay on cold nights,
When the big white folks
Got billions an' billions of dollars in business?

Benjamin Rosenbaum

Benjamin Rosenbaum bought dolls, blonde or brunette,
Carried them to his stuffy bedroom in the Bronx,
Painted them chocolate-brown or black,
And went from door to door in Harlem.

"My dear lady," he would say to a Negro mother,
His Hebrew countenance darkening with melancholy,
"Your people, like mine, have suffered much
In the crucible of racial prejudice.
Therefore, my heart goes out to your people."

While the Negro mother stood hesitant;
Benjamin Rosenbaum would uncover his basket;
And if a dark child with woolly plaits appeared
He would exclaim:
"My dear lady, what a beautiful child!
I am sure that the little miss will want
One of these colored dolls.
Look at them, my dear lady.
Are they not as beautiful as the dolls
Made for little white girls?"

Benjamin Rosenbaum would pocket the money
Somewhat hurriedly and with effusive thanks
Move toward the door. . . .
"I've often said to my wife that I love colored people,
Because they are so friendly and happy."

208

Wu Shang

Wu Shang, lover of elegant phrases,
Hated the laundry work
To which kismet had chained him;
But his trade grew steadily,
Despite his shortcomings,
For his sunny spirit and jeweled philosophy
Charmed dusky customers.

One day an ugly, sooty-black woman
Whose enormous corset was about to burst
Under the strain of the rebellious flesh,
Bristled up to the little laundryman.

Wu Shang, smiling his artless smile, said:
"My dear lady, the time was short and the work was long,
And Wu Shang is humbled to know that the unavoidable delay
Upsets the lady and hides for one moment the beauty of her face."
The ugly, sooty-black woman dropped her angry manner
As if it were a hot poker.

One day a Harlem sweet man,
Hurrying to keep a date with a high-brown,
Strode up and down his laundry,
Wild-eyed and profane.
Wu Shang, unruffled,
Thinking of the vagaries of men,
Finally insinuated:

"A wise man does not reveal his weakness
By hurrying to keep an engagement with a woman,
Though she be thrice beautiful;
And a wise lover is a lover
Who feeds his beloved on guesses."

The Harlem sweet man quieted down,
Clapped Wu Shang on the back, almost prostrating him,
And grinned: "You know yo' stuff 'bout wimins, Wu Shang."

When Wu Shang saw the agony
In the face of Lewis Jackson,
He knew he customer suffered from the torture of tortures.
Little by little, the patient Oriental
Drew the tragedy from Jackson's reluctant lips.

209

"My friend of many years,"
Said Wu Shang,
"It is easier by far to understand the Seven Stars
Than the caprices of a woman,
For the ways of a woman are as changeable as the ways of the wind
And beyond the understanding of seven Buddhas.
A wise man attempts not to change the course of the wind."

The words of Wu Shang
Were a balm of Gilead to his ebony customer's mind.
Gratitude flowed into his eyes.
He nodded,
Said something that Wu Shang's quick ear could not catch,
And walked out . . . silence brooding behind him.

Tito Crouch

I had no sympathy for a poor white man,
Because this is a white man's country
And a white man is free
And a white man doesn't encounter racial barriers
Every time he turns around.

When the Depression engulfed my tailor shop,
It carried me down to a hobo jungle.
There I met Red,
Whose grocery business was washed out
In San Francisco.
Red saved my life when I almost fell from a freight
Coming out of El Paso, Texas.

Sitting before a pine-box fire one night
In a deserted jungle,
Red told me the tragic story of his life.
His grandfather had worked himself to death and died poor.
His father had done the same.
Red had got a start in life
From his winnings in the sweepstakes;
Then the Depression had wiped out everything.
There he was in a stinking jungle,
Penniless as hell,
Telling a black man about his misfortunes.

Red continued bitterly: "Buddy, the man who said
He's the master of his fate and the captain of his soul
Was the biggest liar that ever lived.

"You've heard it said, Buddy.
That this is a white man's country.
Well, I'm a white man, Buddy,
And I'm going to town to get a white man's money
Out of a white man's bank."

Red laughed like hell.
As he started off I got to my feet,
For I was desperate that night.
I'd been three days without a bite.

211

"Your color's against you, Buddy," said Red.
"They'd spot you damn quick."
Red shook hands with me and left,
And my sympathy went out to a poor white man
The first time in my life. . . .
Red was shot down on the town square
With the money in his hand.

Sylvia Wiggins

The Harlem Advocate headlined the tragedy:
"Wife of Prominent Lodge Man Killed in Car with Lover!"

Since I discovered the letter to Sylvia,
Hidden in that old trunk downstairs,
I now understand the woman
Who was my legal mate for ten years.

I am sorry that *The Harlem Advocate*
Dragged out all the skeletons in Sylvia's closet
When she was killed outside Philadelphia
In Jazz Boker's roadster,
But Napoleon Hannibal Speare
Has made a yellow sheet
Out of the respectable weekly inherited
From The Honorable Caesar Speare,
His illustrious father.

I met Sylvia in Little Rock
At a convention of The Patriotic Order of Negro Citizens.
I had worked hard all my life,
Educating myself,
And I was a virtuous young man.
I remember, the first time I kissed Sylvia,
I almost fainted;
And six days later we were married.
Imagine my surprise the very next day
When I overheard this from a traveling salesman:

"Like a kangaroo leaping from spot to spot,
Sylvia springs from one man's arm to another's.
She's had six hot daddies . . . and two husbands:
One in Shreveport and the second in Memphis."
The stranger and the salesman guffawed.
"She's got the third sucker now," said the stranger.

I was good and sore when I reached the house,
But in Sylvia's arms I forgot everything.
I knew I was a fool, but I was helpless.

Supreme Commander Alonzo Bidwell
Promoted me to the Harlem branch of the lodge.
Overnight Sylvia changed.
She made a fool of herself and a laughingstock of me.
Her lovers were below her social status,
And she made no attempt to hide her affairs.
When I took her to task,
She became fanatical and obstructive.
"You have nobody but yourself to blame!" she would scream,
"You have never tried to understand me. Never!"

Since I discovered the letter of Sylvia's first husband
In that old trunk downstairs, I understand her now.
The letter said in part:
"Plagued with an inferiority complex,
You try to make yourself feel important to yourself
By taking sexual mates who will look up to you."

Lionel Bushman

I ain't always been down like this.
I was a businessman once
An' handled plenty of money
Down in the East Texas oil fields.

When the oil come in at Southernville,
The town growed up like a mushroom.
Although the whites stole right an' left from the Negroes,
They had plenty of money floatin' around.
Old man Bruce, an ex-slave,
Bought him a car a block long.
Said he was gonna ride like a big white man
Before he went to meet his God.
I never saw so many dentists
In a town that size in all my life.
They made big hauls puttin' in gold teeth
In place of good natural ones.

Southernville didn't have a single spot
For the colored folks to enjoy themselves.
So I opened Booker T. Hall,
A clean, high-class entertainment rendezvous,
Where a colored man could bring
His sister, his wife, and his mother;
An' there wouldn't be no socializin'
With razors an' pistols.

For the openin' I got the Harlem High Steppers
Out of Dallas an' started with a wow.
Three nights a week I had floor shows,
Thursday was Amateur Night,
Friday was Bank Night,
And Saturday the Barn Dance.

I've heard some say that colored people
Won't support race enterprises.
There's nothin' to that.
I built up a thrivin' business in Southernville
An' made plenty of money.

I had rented out the basement of the Booker T. Hall
To an old white man.
He said he wanted to store things in it.
I did it more to accommodate him
Than anything else.
One day the police broke into the basement
An' found it half full of booze.

Now, that old white man stood up in court
An' swore on the Bible that he never saw me before
An' that he didn't know where the Booker T. Hall was
Till he went down there with the police.
I lost my head an' called him a god-damned liar,
An' they almost lynched me for that.
One night about two A.M. the sheriff took me to the edge of town
An' told me to beat it. He gave me a dollar.
"Good luck," said the sheriff, as if he didn't know what to say.
So you see I ain't always been down like this.

Stanley de Weerd

The dean of Harlem politicians
Walked up Lenox Avenue,
Whistling a sentimental air.
He was a legendary figure along Dark Row,
And its denizens in poolrooms and basement dives
Had helped him mint the coin of his success.

The old bachelor's face was beaming,
For later in the evening
He was to call on Mrs. Priestley,
The gentle widow
Whom he was to diadem with his name.

Near the middle of a block,
De Weerd saw Tony the Greek
Standing in front of a chop suey restaurant;
And the politician sensed that Tony was harboring matters
Of mutual concern.
Arm in arm,
They entered the Chinese place,
Engaging in a byplay of words that hid deeper things.

A broad-featured Oriental in a dinner jacket
Saluted them and led them toward a short row
Of curtained booths at the rear.

"You habe privacy here," smiled the Chinese,
Pulling a dark curtain aside
With a ceremonial gesture. . . .

With a ludicrous salaam and droll apology
To the startled couple
Whose lovemaking he had interrupted,
The Oriental dropped the curtain and moved away,
Mumbling in his native dialect.

But in that fated instant
Stanley De Weerd had glimpsed
The frightened and guilty expression
On Mrs. Priestley's face.

Michael Ramsey

All my youth I read books
Written by white historians for white boys and girls.
I was overawed by the heroic figures
Of Washington and Jefferson and Lincoln.
I was thrilled by the courage of white Americans
At Bunker Hill,
At Lake Erie,
At San Juan Hill,
At Chateau-Thierry.
I held sacred the memories
Of Plymouth Rock,
The Boston Tea Party,
The Covered Wagon,
The Alàmo.
Breathless, I followed the adventures
Of Captain John Smith,
Of Daniel Boone,
Of David Crockett.

But in the midst of it all,
I felt cheated.
When I heard white boys and girls proudly singing,
"My country 'tis of thee,"
My spirit drooped beneath a terrible weight
Of envy and sadness.

In my manhood I discovered precious documents
In dusty archives.
I learned of the patience and the valor of black men
At Bunker Hill,
At Lake Erie,
At San Juan Hill,
At Argonne.

The pageant of the New World passed before me:
Black men matching their brawn and brain
With hostile nature and brutish men . . .
Black men crossing prairies,
Tunneling mountains,
Building bridges and railroads,
Laying the foundations of mighty cities,
Giving the Southland a system of public education,
Guarding the White House in a crisis.

218

I began to breathe . . . to live . . .
Absorbing the romance and reality
Of Toussaint L'Ouverture.
Of Alexander Pushkin,
Of Alexander Dumas,
Of Frederick Douglass,
Of Khama the Good.

In my manhood I join the symphony of democracy.
In my manhood I feel strong and glad.
In my manhood I sing,
"My country 'tis of thee,"
And look the race of men in the eye
And hold my head up
Like any other American
Or citizen of the world.

Ted Carson

The needle-points of the sleety wind
Stung his face
And the cold of the frozen pavement
Crawled up his legs
And a clock in the crowded window of a pawnshop
Struck the midnight hour,
As Ted Carson trudged along
The desolate reach of Lenox Avenue.

Couldn't hear nobody pray, O Lawd,
Couldn't hear nobody pray;
'Way down yonder by maself
Couldn't hear nobody pray. . . .

The yellow oblong of a lighted window
Showed in a third-floor flat.

Ma Gawd, it sho' looks like an invite to a big party—
Makes me think 'bout the blazin' logs in the fireplace
O' ma ole mammy's cabin down in Virginny. . . .

But a bum must not think of a cheering fireplace,
When the cold sky closes in upon him
And the cold pavement makes his feet ache
And the cold wind flows through his coat,
Like red wine passing through his mammy's sieve.

O Gawd, I mustn't think o' red wine, either,
For red wine makes me remember friendly faces;
An' I ain't seen none since I lef' ma ole Virginny home.

I's lookin' down that Lonesome Road
An' wishin' I was dead.
Lookin' down that Lonesome Road
An' wishin' I was dead.
Like Jesus, I ain't got no place
To lay ma weary head.

Ted Carson went down into the subway,
Fingering the solitary nickel in his pocket.
He entered a train going Uptown.
He rode . . . and rode . . . and rode.
He got off. . . .
He boarded a train going Downtown.
He rode . . . and rode . . . and rode. . . .
He rode Uptown and rode Downtown until
The hungry wheels of the subway trains
Had devoured the cold hours
Between midnight and dawn.

Guy Gage

It was not until months after
The initiatory happening in the protecting shadows
Of the old janitor's basement bedroom
That Guy learned the meaning
Of the big five-letter word.

Later, when his playmates became angry with him
And spat the nauseous word at him,
His thin lips quivered
And his eyes burned with repressed tears
And his frail body trembled
With torturing, unreleasable anger;
But his dumb misery
Only made the little animals on the playground
Bold with a savage joy.

Then the boy's heart grew stouter:
He called his tormentors vilely odorous epithets,
And he slit the plump cheek of one with a pocketknife.
After that, his playfellows plagued him
At longer and longer intervals.

But the nice little girls turned up their noses,
And the boys pointed him out to newcomers,
And Guy felt the walls of a terrible loneliness
Pressing in upon him.

As he grew into manhood,
He became more fastidious in his dress
And discovered many new friends in the half-world
That lies between the world of men
And the world of women:
And he even learned to joke with the old janitor
Who had been his teacher that afternoon
In the protecting shadows of the basement bedroom.

Miss Hilda Angoff

Miss Hilda Angoff
Informs everybody she meets
That she is the descendant of Free Negroes
And that her grandfather
Worked with Frederick Douglass and the abolitionists.
Miss Hilda is a librarian.

In her famous lecture,
"Reading and the Harlem Negro,"
Delivered at Mt. Olivet Baptist Church,
Miss Hilda Angoff peered over her nose-glasses
And shot a barbed challenge at her dark hearers.
"How many of you have read
The Ring and the Book and Plato's *Republic?*"

After a dramatic pause,
Learned in the Department of Speech at Teachers College,
She turned to the overawed chairman and said:
"My people perish for lack of knowledge."

Miss Hilda Angoff suggests some immortal classic
To every reader served by the branch library.
Miss Hilda Angoff thinks
The only good writer is a dead one.
The preachers support her.
They remember her veiled threat:
"A preacher who does not support the library
Is not fit to lead the community."

Aunt Hilda

The Harlem sky flings a curtain of rain
Between the solitary window of Aunt Hilda's narrow room
And the decrepit tenement across the rear courtyard . . .
The tenement with its bleary windows
Like the rheumy eyes of an old sot.

Aunt Hilda mumbles to herself
In her rickety rocking chair . . .
Mumbles an immemorial lullaby;
Her palsied hands lie on the withered lap
That has cradled eight of her master's children
And eleven of her own
And six of her children's children.

Aunt Hilda's lap has sent forth the chief characters
In an American tragedy and a comedie humaine.

Aunt Hilda mumbles to herself
In her rickety rocking chair . . .
Mumbles an immemorial lullaby.

And the moving baritone of the wind
And the low soprano of the rain
Shade into a funeral hymn. . . .

Aunt Hilda is an old shoe
Worn out in service
And left in one of life's forgotten corners.

Jonah Emerson

Old Man Starks nicknamed me Jonah
At the Harlem Barber Shop
When I told him I believed the story
Of Jonah and the whale.

Old Man Starks, the atheist,
Wanted to know what Mrs. Jonah said
When her old man stayed away from home all that time
And returned with that ridiculous fish story.

I told Old Man Starks
He missed the difference between
A truth and a fact.

I told Old Man Starks
That I myself had been in the belly of a whale.
So had he himself.
So had every man living or dead.
So had every nation since the dawn of history.

I have been in the belly of despair.
I have been in the sunless bottoms of perplexities.
Out of the troubled waters my soul has cried:
"O God, how long?"

Then came the light of day . . .
The solution of the problem that vexed my spirit.

Old Man Starks nicknamed me Jonah
At the Harlem Barber Shop.
But I say . . . every man is a Jonah!

Old Man Starks

The only democratic institution left in America
Is the common barbershop.
There . . . a man is a man for a' that.

I admit young Emerson
Got a stranglehold on the old man
In that story of Jonah and the whale.
Emerson graduated in philosophy from Harvard:
He's always quoting Santayana.
My diploma's from the University of Hard Knocks.
I've studied nothing but Thomas Paine and *The Book of Experience*.

The very next day young Emerson returned,
And I pinned his shoulders to the mat
When he tried to prove . . .
Quoting Shakespeare and Aristotle and the ologies . . .
The nobility of Man. I told young Emerson a story:

When I was a small boy in Iowa,
My father had a five-hundred-pound sow.
He used to put enough slop in the trough for all the hogs;
But that big, strapping sow would drive the others away,
Gorge her belly, then lie down in the trough and go to sleep.

I told young Emerson
Every hog thinks only of its own belly . . .
And that starvation in a land of plenty
Proves Man is a hog.

Ben Shockley

If a man die,
Shall he live again?

She was a fine old lady of the Old South,
And I went to work in the Big House
When I was left an orphan.

The war had robbed her of everything . . . everything
But her gentleness of spirit.
Whenever she talked about her husband and her son
Killed in Pickett's charge,
She repeated the deathless speech
She had heard Lincoln make at Gettysburg.

The great living room in the Big House
Became sacred then, and I . . . a little afraid.

I worked the farm on a fifty-fifty basis,
And her old age was secure and comfortable.

In her presence,
I never *felt* that I was a servant.
In her presence,
I never *felt* that I was black.
There are noble characters whom a man respects
Without losing his self-respect.

Sometimes,
In the gloaming of the veranda,
She would look beyond me
And the somber Big House
And the somber state of things . . .
And reveal to me her vision:

"Some day
The souls of men,
As well as their bodies,
Will be free!"

If a man die,
Shall he live again?

I hope
And I hope, O God!
The soul of man is immortal
So that I may see again
That fine old lady of the Old South!

Pops Foote

Two tramps slouched on a bench in the park.
The tree at their backs was crooked and bare,
Like a fantastic skeleton with extended arms.

Cheeks empty and pasty-white, hair blond and matted,
The oldish young man was reading a tobacco-spotted newspaper.

Face like cracked anthracite, hands like a weather-cuffed harness,
Pops Foote pulled the gaping brown derby lower
On his corrugated forehead,
So as to shade his watery eyes from the westerly sun.

Pops had been a peon in the Brazos Bottoms.
The stubborn furrows had wasted his best years.
Now he was useless to his masters.

Said the pasty-white young man with the empty cheeks:
"Pops, the President says
The American people need in these trying times
Faith and hope and loyalty."

Pops looked at the westerly sun
And gave his belt a desperate little tug
And stroked his straggly beard reflectively.

Then Pops said in a thin, squeaky voice:
"Son, I's jest wonderin' if the Mistah President
Ever set on a park bench
Hongry enough to eat a piece of shoe leather."

The Underdog

I am the coon, the black bastard,
On the *Queen Mary*,
The United Air Lines,
The Greyhound,
The Twentieth Century Limited.

I am sambo, the shine,
In the St. Regis Iridium,
The Cotton Club,
The Terrace Room of the New Yorker.

I am the nigger, the black son of a bitch,
From the Florida Keys to Caribou, Maine;
From the Golden Gate
To the Statue of Liberty.

I know the deafness of white ears,
The hate of white faces,
The venom of white tongues,
The torture of white hands.

I know the meek
Shall inherit the graves!

In jim crow schools
And jim crow churches,
In the nigger towns
And the Brazos Bottoms,

Along Hollywood Boulevard
And Tobacco Road—
My teachers were Vice and Superstition,
Ignorance and Illiteracy . . .
My pals were TB and Syphilis,
Crime and Hunger.

Sambo, nigger, son of a bitch,
I came from the loins
Of the great white masters.

Kikes and bohunks and wops,
Dagos and niggers and crackers . . .
Starved and lousy,
Blind and stinking—
We fought each other,
Killed each other,
Because the great white masters
Played us against each other.

Then a kike said: *Workers of the world,unite!*
And a dago said: *Let us live!*
And a cracker said: *Ours for us!*
And a nigger said: *Walk together, children!*

WE ARE THE UNDERDOGS
ON A HOT TRAIL!

Appendix

Harlem

Vergil Ragsdale,
Dishwasher poet at Mr. Maranto's café,
Who wrote the epic *An African Tragedy*
Burned as trash by Big Sadie's husband . . .
Vergil Ragsdale, the consumptive,
Gulped down a glass of molten gin,
Leaned tipsily against the bar in Duke Huggins's Subway,
Scanned with fever-bright eyes
The horizon of uncouth black faces,
And declaimed in funereal cadences:

"Harlem, O Harlem,
I shall not see the quiet dawn
When the yellow and brown and black proletarians
Swarm out of stinking dives and firetrap tenements,
Pour through canyon-streets,
Climb Strivers' Row and Sugar Hill,
Erase the liveried flunkies,
And belly laugh in the rich apartments of the Big Niggers.

"I shall not see the unwashed mob
Hoofing the Lindy Hop in Madame Alpha Devine's drawing room,
Guzzling champagne in Banker Calverton's library,
Bouncing their unperfumed butts upon Miss Briffault's silken beds,
Gorging the roast chicken and eclairs in Editor Speare's kitchen.

"Harlem, O Harlem,
City of the Big Niggers,
Graveyard of the Dark Masses,
Soapbox of the Red Apocalypse . . .
I shall be forgotten like you
Beneath the Debris of Oblivion."

Radicals, prizefighters, actors and deacons,
Beggars, politicians, professors and redcaps,
Bulldikers, Babbitts, racketeers and jig-chasers,
Harlots, crapshooters, workers and pink-chasers,
Artists, dicties, Pullman porters and messiahs . . .
The Curator has hung the likensses of all
In *A Gallery of Harlem Portraits*.

Dusky Bards,
Heirs of eons of Comedy and Tragedy,
Pass along the streets and alleys of Harlem
Singing ballads of the dark world:

233

When a man has lost his taste for you,
    Jest leave dat man alone.
Says I . . . a dawg won't eat a bone
    If he don't want de bone.

I likes de Eyetalian . . . I likes de Jew . . .
I likes de Chinaman, but I don't like you.

    Happy days are here again.
    Dat' sho' one great big lie.
    Ain't had a beefsteak in so long
    My belly wants to cry.

Preacher called to bless my home
An' keep it free from strife.
Preacher called to bless my home
An' keep it free from strife.
Now I's got a peaceful home
An' de preacher's got my wife.

White cops sho' will beat you up, littlest thing you do.
Black cops make Black Boy feel proud, but dey'll beat you too.

    Rather be a hobo, Lawd,
    Wid a stinkin' breath
    Dan live in de Big House
    Workin' folks to death.

    My two-timin' Mama says to me:
    Daddy, did I let you down?
    Gonna break dat woman's gawdamn neck
    Befo' I leaves dis town.

    Black Boy, sing an' clown an' dance,
        Strutt yo' low-down nigger stuff.
    White Folks sho' will tip you big
        If you flatters 'em enough.

Diamond Canady
Was stabbed in bed by little Eva Winn.
Deacon Phineas Bloom
Confessed his adultery on his deathbed.

Frederick Judson
Made cigars that pleased General Ulysses Grant.
Soldier Boy
Was decorated by Pancho Villa.
Poker Face Duncan
Killed his rival with a billiard ball.

234

Joshua Granite

During the Black Reconstruction
He served in the legislature of South Carolina;
And he erupted like a volcano
When colorphobes disparaged the black Solons.
Those dark lawgivers were good and bad,
Ignorant and wise,
In his day as in ours.

Yes,
They fixed up the Capitol
With plate-glass mirrors and elegant lounges,
With luxurious desks and magnificent armchairs,
With the splendor of a free bar;
But they also gave the state
The democracy of a public school system
And a republic of the ballot.

Then came the White Scourge,
The hooded terrors of the Ku Klux Klan:
In their wake,
Widows and orphans crazed in a no-man's-land;
In their wake,
Tree-hanging bodies bloated with menace and portent;
In their wake,
Democracy crucified on the Skull of the South.

He stood among the People and statesmen and robber barons
At Ogden, Utah, when the golden spike
Of the Union Pacific was driven.

He knew John Steel, Coal Oil Johnny,
When Venango County, Pennsylvania,
Was a forest of derricks inhabited by fortune hunters:
Millionaires and beggars and ex-preachers,
Laborers and grafters and Magdalens.
He knew Coal Oil Johnny,
When he'd purchase a team and carriage for a drive,
Then present it to the driver;
When he'd rent an entire hotel
For his personal use.
He knew Coal Oil Johnny, after the crash,
When his home was the ditch where he worked.

Marzimmu Heffner

The headline of *The Harlem Advocate* exclaimed:
"Only Living African Slave in Harlem!"

He came from the Coromantees of the Gold Coast;
And, in spite of the drubbings of time and circumstance,
He retains something of the Spartan vigor and grit
That fibered his proud forebears.

He was a boy when his native village was burned in the night
And five slave-raiders overpowered his father, the chief.
Tortured by the disgrace,
His sire attempted suicide.

"We are not Whydahs, nor Nagoes, nor Pawpaws!" said the chief.
"We Coromantees are men . . . free men."

He remembers the infernal journey to the coast,
The ravages of jungle and flood, of famine and beast,
The polluting breaths of swamps, the chilling poisons of uplands,
The vultures that shadowed the coffles.

He remembers the horrors of the Middle Passage,
The victims packed between decks like sardines in a can,
The vertical brassy sun, the shortage of food and water,
The stench and seasickness,
The raw of brutalities and the nepenthe of prayers.

Came then, the epidemic of smallpox;
The captain ordered the diseased slaves to be thrown overboard
And the others brought, unshackled, upon deck,
Where some were forced to work with the diminished crew.

Cato Snoddy

Often he saw Birdella pass
The Harlem Jewelry Store.
Where he worked as porter;
And on each occasion he found himself in need of her
With a want that hurt.

One evening he went with Gloomy Dean
To a chicken dinner served by The Ladies' Aid,
And there he came face to face with Birdella,
The soloist in St. Luke's M. E. Church.

After their hasty marriage,
Cato would not let his wife work for old Mrs. Van Buren
In the little antique shop on MacDougal Street.

Cato wanted his wife to have a career.
He insisted that she study under Professor Dos Passos,
The most famous teacher of voice in Harlem.

Cato strutted up Seventh Avenue with his wife,
And boasted of her good looks and talent,
And bought her, on the installment plan, a glittering tiara
To be worn at her first recital. . . . Three years rolled by.

It was cold and blustery in the street,
But the Harlem Opera House was pleasant.
An air of expectancy hung in the old theater.
At the piano sat Professor Dos Passos,
His long fingers tapping his knees nervously,
His eyes cocked at one of the wings on the stage.

The audience cheered wildly
When Madam Birdella Dos Passos, recently arrived from Paris,
Swept majestically across the stage in her white satin gown,
Leaving the audience breathless with her glittering tiara.

Cato Snoddy, slumped in a dark box, all alone,
Emptied his flask with one long draught.
Then, standing up unnoticed,
He took deliberate aim and hurled the bottle at his ex-wife.
It struck the piano and flew in pieces.
Professor Dos Passos let out a yell of dismay.
Frightened, Madame Birdella started for the wings.
A great murmur, like a flock of unrushing blackbirds,
Rose in the Harlem Opera House.
Cato Snoddy slumped in the dark box . . . dead drunk.

Melvin B. Tolson

Charles S. Johnson, E. Franklin Frazier, Rudolph Fisher, Herbert Delaney, Melvin B. Tolson

The New Negro on the march

Three "Gay Northeasterners" on Seventh Avenue

Looking in the icebox

Fireside memories

244

Jitterbugging at the Savoy

Paul Robeson as Emperor Jones

Charles Gilpin as Emperor Jones 247

Bessie Smith

. . . and then there was Prohibition

W. E. B. Du Bois

Marcus Garvey

Couple in racoon coats

Honoring the president of the Republic of Liberia

254

Afterword
by Robert M. Farnsworth

The artist

is

a zinnia

no

first frost

blackens with a cloven hoof;

an eyeglass

—in the eye of a dusty wind—

to study the crosses and tangles in warp and woof;

an evergreen cherry

parasitic upon a winter sun;

a paltry thing with varicose veins

when the twelve fatigues are done. *

Melvin B. Tolson's birth date, February 6, 1898, is not far from the birth date of the twentieth century. As a social activist, teacher, scholar, and poet Tolson was intensely self-conscious about positioning himself in the flux of history. Retrospectively it is clear that Tolson just missed some of the major fashions in cultural history. Born of the same generation of many of the writers of the Harlem Renaissance, he did not begin to publish until the 1930s. Later, absorbing the difficult theses of modernism of T. S. Eliot and the New Criticism, but very conscious of racial and cultural ironies that distanced him from them, he worked out an extraordinarily complex style of his own, assimilating modernist techniques to the needs of black American experience, just as Eliot and the New Criticism began to wane as dominant forces in literary fashion. Such changes may have left him momentarily out of step, but Tolson's true place in literary history, the accuracy and penetration of his vision and the richness and technical mastery of his achievement, has by no means yet been carefully and thoroughly assessed.

Melvin B. Tolson's literary reputation depends principally upon his last published book-length poem, *The Harlem Gallery, Book I: The Curator*. In his introduction to *Harlem Gallery*, Karl Shapiro claims

*The Harlem Gallery.

with much justice, "A great poet has been living in our midst for decades and is almost totally unknown, even by the literati, even by poets."[1] Roy P. Basler, writing eight years later, asks a rhetorical question, "What American poet will symbolize and represent our milieu to readers in the future, as Shakespeare represents the Elizabethan, Milton the Puritan, or, to come closer, Whitman the Civil War era?" He answers as follows:

> It is not *The Waste Land* or *Four Quartets*, I think, which limn the present or light the future with the past so well that scholars salvaging libraries of this era may someday guess what manner of men were we. Nor is it even Sandburg's *The People, Yes*, nor William Carlos Williams' *Paterson*, but Tolson's *The Harlem Gallery*, rather, where the heart of blackness with the heart of whiteness lies revealed. Man, what do you think you are is not the white man's question but the black man's rhetorical answer to the white man's question. No poet in the English language, I think, has brought larger scope of mind to greater depth of heart than Melvin Tolson in his unfinished song to the soul of humanity.[2]

These are extravagant claims, yet because Melvin Tolson's' achievement is too little known and understood, their extravagance has not been, and perhaps at present cannot be, accurately measured. Critics and readers have been ducking the challenge of his work for years except for a few who have been willing to let loose some critical haymakers. Extravagant, perhaps. Yet these haymakers may well be right on the mark.

Harlem Gallery is an extraordinary poem that has not been adequately critically examined and evaluated in print. There have been several appreciative comments. And some useful attempts at explication. Among the most useful are Joy Flasch's chapter in her book-length study of Tolson[3] and the unpublished critical edition of *Harlem Gallery* that Robert J. Huot prepared for his doctoral dissertation.[4] Extensive critical scholarship will be necessary to fill in the lacuna between the modest critical efforts at explication and the extravagant possibilities that able critics and poets have sensed in the poem. Such criticism needs to be based on an understanding of the entire range of Tolson's writing, which covers a long period of literary and biographical history and which consistently challenges deeply in-

1. Melvin B. Tolson, *The Harlem Gallery, Book I: The Curator* (New York: Twayne Publishers, Inc., 1965), p. 11.

2. Roy P. Basler, "The Heart of Blackness—M. B. Tolson's Poetry," *New Letters* (Spring 1973), p. 73.

3. Joy Flasch, *Melvin B. Tolson* (New York: Twayne Publishers, Inc., 1972), pp. 99–133.

4. Robert J. Huot, "Melvin B. Tolson's *Harlem Gallery*: A Critical Edition with Introduction and Explanatory Notes," Ph.D. dissertation, University of Utah, August 1971.

grained but often unwitting racial and cultural biases of the American literary establishment.

The publication here for the first time of *A Gallery of Harlem Portraits*, Tolson's first book-length manuscript of poems, should significantly help scholar-critics to an understanding and accurate critical appraisal of Tolson's poetic achievement. This manuscript, probably completed about 1935, is Tolson's first attempt to put the life of Harlem into ambitious poetic form. It is a long but significant journey of intellectual and poetic development from this manuscript to *Harlem Gallery*, published in 1965. The latter is elaborately urbane and filled with esoteric wit, both learned and folk. The former is relatively crude, but often strong and immediate in its impact. *Harlem Gallery* is intricately organized. *A Gallery of Harlem Portraits* is loose and sprawling. *Harlem Gallery* probes with mockingly penetrating humor and irony into questions about the essential nature of man and the significance in his life of the concepts of race and art. *A Gallery of Harlem Portraits* presents brief dramatic portraits of life in Harlem much more simply and directly, without the elaborately reflective dialogues of characters such as The Curator and Doctor Nkomo. In *Harlem Gallery* Doctor Nkomo observes that "life and art beget incestuously." He and The Curator, the protagonist of the poem, like Ishmael and an African Socrates, lament and probe the cultural dilemmas posed by the aspirations and responsibilities of art complicated by the provocative absurdities and opportunities of being both African and American. Their dialogue is stimulated and pointed by the poems within the poem produced by the characters, John Laugart and Hideho Heights. In *A Gallery* the art of the poet is meant to be unobtrusive, only a facilitating agent for rendering the life of Harlem with dramatic intensity. *A Gallery* is much less cerebral, much less artistically self-conscious. It gives pleasure more simply and appeals more readily to a sense of social justice.

In 1930 Tolson began work on a master's degree at Columbia University. The stock-market crash of 1929 and the ensuing bitter economic depression were bringing down a fast curtain on the Harlem Renaissance. Much of the exotic glitter of Harlem as a fashionable playground for wealthy and sophisticated whites and as a promise of a quick and glamorous entry into the American Dream for blacks was wiped away. Harlem awoke with a proletarian morning-after headache. Harlem awoke with the blues. But the vividness of the good times and the promise of the twenties were not completely obliterated. They were too real, too close, to be forgotten. Harlem was still vital and full of ironies to be explored. In his master's thesis Tolson pays tribute to the writers of the Renaissance with whom he had become personally acquainted and who were in age his contemporaries. Claude McKay was nine years older; Rudolph Fisher, three; Eric Walrond, two. Sterling Brown and Zora Neale Hurston were one year younger; Langston

Hughes and Wallace Thurman, two; and Countee Cullen, three. Harlem had embraced them all.

Portentous economic events had changed Harlem, but Harlem would always be the cultural capital of black America for Tolson. Hard times ironically brought Harlem closer to Tolson. Tolson maintained a teaching position at Wiley College throughout the depression, but his pay was always minimal. Sometime in the thirties, he actively organized sharecroppers, both white and black, in southeastern Texas. He protected his wife and family from the details of his activities, but they knew he was involved. His experiences with economic hardship and exploitation made him a Marxist. He read *New Masses* regularly, and he formed a close personal and professional friendship at Wiley with Oliver Cromwell Cox, who in his introduction to *Caste, Class, and Race* expressed his gratitude particularly to his colleagues: "Professors Melvin B. Tolson, Andrew P. Watson, V. E. Daniel, and Alonzo J. Davis." Probably just after completing *A Gallery of Harlem Portraits*, Tolson formed another close personal and professional friendship with V. F. Calverton, the radically iconoclastic editor of *Modern Quarterly* who published several poems from *A Gallery*.[5]

Tolson himself has left a vivid literary description of the inception of *A Gallery of Harlem Portraits*:

> In 1932 [sic] I was a Negro poet writing Anglo-Saxon sonnets as a graduate student in an Eastern University. I moved in a world of twilight haunted by the ghosts of a dead classicism. My best friend there was a German-American who'd sold stories to the magazines. We read each other's manuscripts and discussed art, science and literature instead of cramming for the examinations. My ignorance of contemporary writers was abysmal.
>
> One cold wet afternoon the German-American read my sonnet Harlem, cleared his throat, and said: "It's good, damned good, but—"
>
> The word "but" suspended me in space. I could hear the clock on the desk; its tick-tock, tick-tock, swelled into the pounding of a sledgehammer on an iron plate. The brutal words knifed into my consciousness: "You're like the professors. You think the only good poet is a *dead* one. Why don't you read Sandberg, Masters, Frost, Robinson? Harlem is too big, too lusty, for a

5. Joy Flasch indicates that Tolson met Calverton in 1930, *Melvin B. Tolson*, "Chronology," p. 15. In an interview with me June 23, 1978, in Washington, D. C., James Farmer was quite certain that Tolson met Calverton for the first time when the latter visited Wiley to judge an intercollegiate dramatic competition. Farmer was the student representative at the time who had invited Calverton to come. He also subsequently became a close friend of Calverton's. However, a letter from V. F. Calverton to Tolson dated November 23, 1937, now in the possession of Dr. Arthur Tolson, begins, "It was damn swell meeting you the other day and I do hope your conference with Cerf was inspiring." The rest of the letter suggests a new acquaintance.

sonnet. Say, we've never had a Negro epic in America. Damn it, you ought to stop piddling!"

I placed the sonnet at the beginning of my thesis on the Harlem Renaissance. Under the painstaking supervision of Dr. Arthur Christy I had learned the beauty of the inevitable word.

At the end of four years and 20,000 miles of traveling and the wasting of 5,000 sheets of paper, I had finished the epic *A Gallery of Harlem Portraits*.[6]

The sonnet Tolson refers to is not now included in the copy of his master's thesis retained at Columbia University; however, there is not much doubt that the Harlem of *A Gallery of Harlem Portraits* is bigger and lustier than that described in the lost sonnet. It may be pretentious to refer to it as an epic, as Tolson does above, but epic is what Tolson believed Harlem deserved and *A Gallery* is unquestionably a significant step toward the uncompleted epic that he ultimately projected almost thirty years later in *Harlem Gallery*. Regrettably Tolson was able to complete only *Book I: The Curator* before his death. Book II was to be titled *Egypt Land*; Book III, *The Red Sea*; Book IV, *The Wilderness*; and Book V, *The Promised Land*. After presenting the contemporary picture of Harlem in Book I, Tolson intended to use the biblical metaphors claimed by black Americans for generations as a narrative pattern to describe the hegira of blacks through the experience of cultural dislocation and racial slavery to the promise of freedom and cultural self-realization. The achievement of Book I suggests that it would have been an extraordinary epic indeed. Remarking on Book I, Tolson indicates something of the larger schema he had in mind: "A poet, consciously or unconsciously, etches the differentiae of his time. *The Gallery* is an attempt to picture the Negro in America before he becomes the great auk of the melting-pot in the dawn of the twenty-second century."[7]

Harlem was a seed that grew and flourished in Tolson's literary imagination. To indicate and clarify the stages of that development and the literary influences and insights that nurtured it with completeness is too ambitious a task for this afterword. But the importance of *A Gallery of Harlem Portraits* as a stage in this development can at least be indicated.

The seed's germination is evident in Tolson's thesis on Renaissance writers:

> Harlem is the unique product of New York City as the meeting-place of races and cultures in the Western Hemisphere. Sociologists and fictionists have made intensive and

6. Tolson Manuscripts, Library of Congress. This story is also repeated with slight variations in "*Melvin B. Tolson*: An Interview," *Anger, and Beyond: The Negro Writer in the United States* (New York: Harper & Row, Inc., 1966), p. 194.

7. Notebook, Tolson Manuscripts, Library of Congress.

extensive studies of the metropolis within a metropolis which have revealed, to eyes familiar only with ante-bellum and post-bellum stereotypes, an El Dorado of racial dissimilarities, varying from the low life characters of the rebel Jamaican's naturalistic *Home to Harlem* to the dark intelligentsia of *Portraits in Color*.[8]

The cultural and ethnic diversity of Harlem fascinated Tolson for both personal and cultural reasons. In "The Olyssey of a Manuscript" Tolson indicated that he felt particularly close to his mother. She told him tales of black heroes, poets, and artists. She encouraged his aspirations and even made him feel obligated to write as a fulfillment of her own dreams, or at least this is as Tolson remembers it. This "little walnut-hued woman was fiercely proud of being an American Negro, although in her veins flowed Irish, French, Indian, and African blood."[9] As her son, Tolson too was fiercely proud of his black heritage, but he was also keenly aware of the diversity of his own ethnic and racial heritage. Harlem, "the meeting place of races and cultures in the Western Hemisphere," was always a cultural home in Tolson's imagination.

Cultural fusion of race and class continued to fascinate and preoccupy Tolson throughout his life. The character of The Curator, the protagonist of *Harlem Gallery* suggests the continued importance of this theme for Tolson:

> The Curator is of Afroirishjewish ancestry. He is an octoroon, who is a Negro in New York and a white man in Mississippi. Like Walter White, the late executive of the N.A.A.C.P., and the author of *A Man Called White*, the Curator is a "voluntary" Negro. Hundreds of thousands of Octoroons like him have vanished in the Caucasian race—never to return. This is a great joke among Negroes. So Negroes ask the rhetorical question, "What man is white?" We never know the real name of the Curator. The Curator is both physiologically and psychologically "The Invisible Man." He as well as his darker brothers, think in Negro. Book One is his autobiography. He is a cosmopolite, a humanist, a connoisseur of the fine arts, with catholicity of taste and interest. He knows intimately lowbrows and middlebrows and highbrows.[10]

In his master's thesis Tolson saw the Harlem Renaissance primarily as the cultural expression of the New Negro as Alain Locke described him, but he also noted the fascination of the Negro for white writers and publishers. Thus Tolson, along with such Renaissance writers as Langston Hughes and Jean Toomer, was encouraged to see

8. "The Harlem Group of Negro Writers," M. A. Thesis, Columbia University (June 1940), p. 7.

9. "The Odyssey of a Manuscript," Tolson Manuscripts, Library of Congress.

10. Cut B, manuscript of a tape made for the University of Wisconsin educational radio station, March 10, 1965. Quoted by Flasch, *Melvin B. Tolson*, p. 100.

the Negro with all his cultural diversity, not just as a new development in the exclusive racial history of black Americans but as both test and promise of the American Dream. The New Negro held the promise of being a New American.

Chester Himes expressed the persistence of this promise with a scorn for the patronizing "primitive" stereotype, a scorn that Tolson would have found congenial, even though he probably would have differed on other expressions of personal taste:

> Obviously and unavoidably, the American black man is the most neurotic, complicated, schizophrenic, unanalyzed, anthropologically advanced specimen of mankind in the history of the world. The American black is a new race of man to come into being in modern time. And for those hackneyed, diehard, outdated, slaverytime racists to keep thinking of him as a primitive is an insult to the intelligence. In fact, intelligence isn't required to know the black is a new man—complex, intriguing, and not particularly likable. I find it very difficult to like American blacks myself; but I know there's nothing primitive about us.[11]

A Gallery of Harlem Portraits reveals Tolson's early fascination with Harlem's "El Dorado of racial dissimilarities." He does not generalize ambitiously about the significance of this cultural diversity as he will later in *Harlem Gallery, Book I*. At this point, he makes no great claims explicitly, but there is implicit pride in his fascination. He dramatizes the lives of Harlem people very directly and immediately so that the reader experiences the joys and pains, the frustrations and intensity, the impoverishment and the ingenuity, in short the style of Harlem life.

Tolson frequently used the public world of the Harlem Renaissance in drawing his portraits, but he usually deliberately altered names and specific biographical information so that his portraits became generalized or "type" figures rather than incisive comments on particular personalities. The portrait of "Madame Alpha Devine," for example, is almost certainly based on the life of Madame C. J. Walker, whose success in the cosmetics business made her both famous and rich, although specific biographical details are deliberately altered. "Abraham Dumas" is a fictionalized picture of Alain Locke. There are numerous veiled literary references as well. I suspect that "Simon Southorn" is a disguised comment on Jean Toomer's *Cane*. It is perhaps relevant to note that Tolson surprisingly ignores Toomer in his master's thesis. "Willie Byrd" seems a character cut from the same cloth as McKay's Banjo. While trying out an exaggeratedly poetic style in "Percy Longfellow" Tolson may have attempted to parody the poetic elegance of Countee Cullen. Several other portraits—"Miss Felicia

11. Chester Himes, *The Quality of Hurt: The Autobiography of Chester Himes, Volume I* (New York: Doubleday & Co., 1972), pp. 285–86.

Babcock," "Grand Chancellor Knapp Sackville," "Napoleon Hannibal Speare," "Elbert Hartman," "Ray Rosenfeld," "Xavier van Loon," "Winged Feet Cooper," and others—teasingly suggest real historical prototypes. "The Reverend Isaiah Cloud" is almost certainly an idealized fantasy self-projection. The preaching tradition is strong in Tolson's family. He always saw himself as a penetrating truth seeker, one who saw through the pretentions of wealth and position. He assimilated something of the twenties' free-spirited artistic scorn of the vulgar middle class as well as the thirties' more indignant sense of the injustice of the distribution of wealth. And he saw both snobbery and economic exploitation as deeply infused with racism. He also was neither surprised nor discouraged when the world never seemed to want to hear about the truth that he saw.

The typescript of *A Gallery of Harlem Portraits* suggests that the opening poem, "Harlem," may well have been written later than the other portraits in an attempt to give the entire book focus and some coherence. It only partially succeeds, but the effort indicates the direction in which Tolson's imagination is later to develop *Harlem Gallery*, *Book I*. In "Harlem," Vergil Ragsdale, consumptive poet working as a dishwasher, has written an epic poem, "An African Tragedy." Acknowledging his own rapidly approaching death, he sketches roughly the historical transformation of Harlem that he will not live to observe. This editorial gnomic observation follows:

> The Curator has hung the likenesses of all
> In *A Gallery of Harlem Portraits*

The character of The Curator is not developed in this poem or anywhere else in this manuscript. There *is* a later poem-portrait of Vergil Ragsdale. Ragsdale's role in this manuscript suggests the roles to be played in the later *Harlem Gallery* by Mister Starks, the suicide musician poet, author of *Harlem Vignettes*, and Hideho Heights who gives the bravura public tributes to John Henry and Louis ("Satchmo") Armstrong, but whose more ambitious and private poem, *E. & O. E.* so moves and disturbs The Curator—the latter reference is an oblique advertisement for Tolson's own critically neglected poem by the same name.

In *A Gallery*, probably under the influence of *Spoon River Anthology*, the concept of a series of poetic portraits is kept relatively simple and the formal implications of the relation between poetry and painting are left relatively unexamined. In *Harlem Gallery*, Hideho Heights challengingly declares that in the beginning was the word, but The Curator, an ex-professor of art, along with the trenchant African, Doctor Nkomo, persist in trying to reconcile the claims of painter, poet, and musician, as artists who clarify and give meaning to the profusion and confusion of human experience in any historical time.

The story of Big Sadie's role in destroying Ragsdale's manuscripts after his death seems a probable source for the later version of Big Mama's role in preserving Mister Starks's *Harlem Vignettes* for The Curator's guardianship. But again we see an elaborate structure develop from a simple pathetic incident. Prince Banmurji is also a possible prototype of the later and more richly developed Doctor Obi Nkomo.

Two poems from *A Gallery* were revised and combined to appear in *Voices* in 1950.[12] The two poems, "African China" and "Wu Shang," are combined under the title of the former. Wu Shang, a Chinese laundryman in Harlem, is a man of quick perception and enigmatic eloquence. He and Dixie Dixon of the revised poem, or Mabel of the earlier version, marry and have a son named African China. This revision is additional evidence that Harlem continued very much in Tolson's mind, "the unique product of New York City as the meeting-place of races and cultures in the Western Hemisphere."

Tolson has recalled some of the early literary influences that give impetus and form to his first book of poems:

> The first finished manuscript of the Harlem Gallery [*A Gallery of Harlem Portraits*] was written in free verse. That was the fashion introduced by the imagists. It contained 340 pages. *The Spoon River Anthology* of Edgar Lee Masters was my model. Browning's psychology in characterization stimulated me. I had deserted the great Romantics and Victorians. Walt Whitman's exuberance was in the marrow of my bones.[13]

If the influence of Masters, Browning, and Whitman are all readily apparent in *A Gallery*, there is yet another, and probably even more important, unacknowledged influence.

The blues is such an implicit part of Tolson's experience and writing that at the time of making the above statement, it apparently did not warrant his conscious recognition. However, in his master's thesis he identifies the particular poetic achievement of Langston Hughes, who in "The Weary Blues" "catches the undercurrent of philosophy that pulses through the soul of the Blues singer and brings the Blues rhythms into American versification."[14] The reader by means of the blues form can "experience the utter physical and mental fatigue of the Negro after the cruel sleeplessness of the night-hours, facing the desolate flatness of another day." This use of the blues indicates to Tolson that Hughes "understands the tragedy of the dark masses whose laughter is a dark laughter."[15] The profound racial message of the blues carries for Tolson, as it did for Hughes, significant proletarian over-

12. Tolson, "African China," *Voices* no. 140 (Winter 1950): 35–38. This poem has since been reprinted in *Kaleidoscope*, ed. Robert Hayden and *Blackamerican Literature*, ed. Ruth Miller.

13. Herbert Hill, ed., "Melvin B. Tolson: An Interview," *Anger, and Beyond: The Negro Writer in the United States*, pp. 194–95.

14. Tolson, "The Harlem Group of Negro Writers," p. 37.

15. Ibid., p. 38.

tones. The dark laughter of the blues permeates *A Gallery of Harlem Portraits* as well.

In *Blues People* Le Roi Jones calls his reader's attention to:

> the beginning of blues as one beginning of American Negroes. Or, let me say, the reaction and subsequent relation of the Negro's experience in this country in *his* English is one beginning of the Negro's *conscious* appearance on the American scene. . . . There were no formal stories about the Negro's existence in America passed down in any pure African tongue. The stories, myths, moral examples, etc., given in African were about Africa. When America became important enough to the African to be passed on, in those *formal* renditions, to the young, those renditions were in some kind of Afro-American language. And finally, when a man looked up in some anonymous field and shouted, "Oh Ahm tired a dis mess, / Oh, yes, Ahm so tired a dis mess," you can be sure he was an American.[16]

Jones describes the "classic blues" that became prominent during the Harlem Renaissance as, "the first Negro music that appeared in a formal context as entertainment, though it still contained the harsh, uncompromising reality of the earlier blues forms. It was, in effect, the perfect balance between the two worlds, and as such, it represented a clearly definable step by the Negro back into the mainstream of American society."[17] By affirming the Negro's sense of being a part of a particular society, the blues also afforded him an opportunity to express racial or ethnic experiences that paradoxically held the promise of universality: "Perhaps what is so apparent in classic blues is the sense for the first time that the Negro felt he was a part of that superstructure of American society at all. The lyrics of classic blues became concerned with situations and ideas that are recognizable as having issued from one area of a much larger concern . . . . Classic blues attempts a universality that earlier blues could not even envision."[18]

The introductory poem of *A Gallery of Harlem Portraits* looks forward to the later *Harlem Gallery* by emphasizing the universality of the Harlem experience:

Dusky Bards,
Heirs of eons of Comedy and Tragedy,
Pass along the streets and alleys of Harlem
Singing ballads of the dark world:
Then Tolson switches directly into a blues lyric:
>When a man has lost his taste for you,
>>Jest leave dat man alone.
>>Says I . . . a dawg won't eat a bone

16. Le Roi Jones, *Blues People: Negro Music and White America* (New York: Apollo Editions, Inc., 1963), p. xii.
17. Ibid., p. 86.
18. Ibid., p. 87.

If he don't want de bone.
I likes de Eyetalian . . . I likes de Jew . . .
I likes de Chinaman, but I don't like you.
  Happy days are here again.
  Dat's sho' one great big lie.
  Ain't had a beefsteak in so long
  My belly wants to cry.

Preacher called to bless my home
An' keep it free from strife
Preacher called to bless my home
An' keep it free from strife.
Now I's got a peaceful home
An' de preacher's got my wife.

White cops sho' will beat you up, littlest thing you do.
Black cops make Black Boy feel proud, but dey'll beat you too.

  Rather be a hobo, Lawd,
  Wid a stinkin' breath
  Dan live in de Big House
  Workin' folks to death.

My two-timin' Mama says to me:
Daddy, did I let you down?
Gonna break dat woman's gawddamn neck
Befo' I leaves dis town.

Black Boy, sing an' clown an' dance,
  Strutt yo' low-down nigger stuff.
White Folks sho' will tip you big
  If you flatters 'em enough.

The poem then closes with a brief and incomplete list of blues experiences that are the subjects of later poems in the manuscript.

Years later in the opening section of *Harlem Gallery* Tolson will again invoke the blues experience:

As a Hambletonian gathers his legs for a leap,
    dead wool and fleece wool
I have mustered up from hands
    now warm or cold: a full
    rich Indies' cargo;
but often I hear a dry husk-of-locust blues
descend the tone ladder of a laughing goose,
    syncopating between
    the faggot and the noose:
    "Black Boy, O Black Boy,
is the port worth the cruise?"

The blues, however, in the later poem are incorporated into a more symphonic idiom and structure. The stories of John Laugart and Mister Starks are blues stories, but they are not given in the more readily

265

recognizable blues idiom so frequently used in *A Gallery of Harlem Portraits*.

The blues root Tolson's poetry in the experience of black America, and they provide a literary means of expressing some of his most deeply felt social contradictions. He is fascinated with cultural fusion, and he sees in the Harlem experience a cultural pluralism and sophistication of extraordinary promise. But the dark laughter is always there, a sometimes bitter but strangely tonic laughter that keeps the painful but fortifying awareness of the history of the black American ever present even in the most optimistic and imaginative speculations on his future.

A few of the poems in *A Gallery* may also surprise Tolson readers with their blatant political propaganda. Tolson described himself throughout his life as a Marxist, yet placed against the background of such poems as *The Libretto* and *Harlem Gallery* such a self-definition seems almost idiosyncratic. Tolson never joined any of the Communist or Socialist parties. As mayor of Langston in the fifties, and probably much earlier in his life, he was an active Democrat. He always prized and protected his independence as a writer. He was deeply suspicious of submitting his talents to the discipline of any group or party. Yet he had personally experienced gross class and racial injustice. "The Ballad of a Rattlesnake" in *Rendezvous with America* is a powerful reminder of Tolson's experiences organizing sharecroppers. Two poems in this manuscript, "Zip Lightner" and "Uncle Gropper," are products of these same experiences. And "Lionel Bushman," "Big Jim Casey," "Edna Borland," "Freemon Hawthorne," "Ted Carson," and the closing poem, "The Underdog," underscore Tolson's deep social concern.

During the forties, and certainly by the fifties, Marxism became for Tolson more a set of intellectual assumptions about the nature of history than a particular political discipline. His position in the early sixties is vividly indicated in a letter to Benjamin F. Bell, Jr., December 28, 1961:

> Ideas sift down, Marx and Lenin and Castro were not of the masses but *for* the masses. What does a Cuban peon know about *Das Kapital*? If you gave him a copy, he'd wipe his behind with it! Well, a peon has to use *some* kind of paper. What's better than that you can't read. There is not a greater strategist on the Left than Old Man Du Bois. He always catches the Wall Street Boys with their pants down and their backs bent at the proper angle. I admire the Toe Groza of the Cleveland Browns. Who is a better place-kicker? Only Old Man Du Bois. Joined the Party at 93! Now mind you, he's in Africa writing a Negro encyclopedia! *Jet* says he's the most popular Negro in Africa! Lawd, Lawd, Lawd!

Some of the poems in *A Gallery* suggest that Tolson was not so certain in the thirties as he was in the sixties of the relation between art and politics. A poem as propagandistically banal as "Hilmar Enick"

266

can hardly be defended on any grounds, but scattered through the latter portion of the manuscript there are a few tired poems, and not all of them are concerned with political sermonizing. "Harold Lincoln," for example, is also deadly flat. Fortunately, these poems are few and far between.

During the late thirties and early forties ethnic references were apt to be more blatant caricatures than we find comfortable today. Calverton, for example, when he published the final poem of *A Gallery*, which Tolson titled, "The Underdog," changed the title to a brassy, "Kikes, Bohunks, Crackers, Dagos, Niggers."[19] This may be a matter of particular sensitivity since we live in a time when the full horror of the Holocaust has been documented and revealed. Tolson's stereotypic portraits of Jews include anti-Semitic biases that were then so common that they could be projected with considerable personal innocence. It should be noted that by 1939 Tolson had finished a novel, *The Lion and the Jackal*, which showed that he was very sensitive to the threat that Hitler and fascism posed, and he saw clearly the links between the murderous treatment of Jews and of blacks.

One cannot help but be struck by the variety of topical references in *A Gallery of Harlem Portraits*. The thirties were a period of intellectual stretching and testing for Tolson, but he was also acutely interested in the changes that were occurring in the American social fabric. At Wiley College he was a phenomenally successful debate coach, drilling his students relentlessly on all the possible arguments related to some of the major issues of the day. He was in great demand as a public speaker, and the topics ranged far beyond the literary. From November 20, 1937, to May 15, 1943, Tolson published a weekly column in the Washington, D.C., *Tribune* titled "Caviar and Cabbage." In it he spoke out freely and forcefully on a great miscellany of social issues. *A Gallery* reflects the commitment of a passionately engaged, if often whimsically ironic imagination. But it is characteristic of Tolson's political position that when Calverton was attacked by *New Masses*, it never troubled their friendship. Tolson's political beliefs hung loosely around his strong personal loyalties.

Melvin Tolson taught all of his adult life in black schools—Wiley College, Langston and Tuskegee universities. He always lived within black communities. He seldom felt the need consciously to proclaim his blackness. Instead he feared and struggled against provincialism. Some of his public statements, by emphasizing the importance of what was happening in the literary world at large, have misled some of his critics into thinking that he was so fascinated with white writers and their achievement that he lost touch with black people. For instance, impressed by T. S. Eliot's winning the Nobel Prize in 1948, Tolson

19. Tolson, "Kikes, Bohunks, Crackers, Dagos, Niggers," *The Modern Quarterly* 11:4 (Autumn 1939): 18–19.

prepared a commencement address which announced a program for a "New Negro Poetry for the New Negro":

> The standard of poetry has changed completely. Negroes must become aware of this. This is the age of T. S. Eliot who just won the Nobel Prize in Literature. If you know Shakespeare from A to Z, it does not mean you can read one line of T. S. Eliot! . . . Imitation must be in technique only. We have a rich heritage of folk lore and history. We are a part of America. We are a part of the world. Our native symbols must be lifted into the universal. Yes, we must study the techniques of Robert Lowell, Dylan Thomas, Carlos Williams, Ezra Pound, Karl Shapiro, W. H. Auden. The greatest revolution has not been in science, but in poetry. We must study such magazines as *Partisan Review*, the *Sewanee Review*, *Accent* and the *Virginia Quarterly*. We must read such critics as Crowe Ransom, Allen Tate, Stephen Spender, George Dillon and Kenneth Burke.[20]

Underneath the rather conventional academic admonitions is the sly smile of the conjure poet: "Imitation must be in technique only. We have a rich heritage of folk lore and history. We are a part of America. We are a part of the world. Our native symbols must be lifted into the universal." In his journal Tolson noted:

> At one time Mr. Eliot was the nigger of poetry; so he had to walk hard and talk loud. See essay on Milton—the first; then the last. Look how Pound attacked Shakespeare's "multitudinous seas incarnadine."
> Eliot antithesizes in order to synthesize—that is the root of thinking—which is establishing a definite relation between ideas or groups of ideas. . . .
> I shall visit a land unvisited by Mr. Eliot.
> I admire Mr. Eliot's honesty. He is a Christian: an open confession is good for the soul—and also society. For thousands of years poets have been thieves. Shakespeare admitted his guilt. Mr. Eliot not only admitted his but in the notes told us exactly where we could find the stolen goods.[21]

Joy Flasch quotes from a letter Tolson wrote to a friend in 1961: "My work is certainly difficult in metaphors, symbols, and juxtaposed ideas. There the similarity between Eliot and me separates . . . when you look at my ideas and Eliot's, we're as far apart as hell and heaven."[22] There is perhaps a slight hint of the dark laughter of the blues in the humor with which place is identified with author.

Tolson saw himself as leading black poetry into a modern period that was being shaped by nonracial historical forces, and he was both jeal-

20. Quoted by Flasch, *Melvin B. Tolson*, p. 70.
21. Tolson, "Quotes and Unquotes on Poetry," *Kansas Quarterly* (Summer 1975): 37.
22. Flasch, *Melvin B. Tolson*, p. 135.

268

ous and confident about it. There is a revealing self-descriptive note among his manuscripts at the Library of Congress, which reads as if it were intended as PR information for *Harlem Gallery*:

> M. B. Tolson dips into varied experiences beginning in Harlem, as a college student in [the] 20's & 30's, his Columbia University study of the Harlem Renaissance later, and from them emerges this graphic picture of the Curator of the Harlem Gallery and the inimitable Zulu Club Wits. Against a background of artists, poets, singer[s], blues, jazz, and the Negro avant-garde, Tolson, *the Father of Negro poetry in the modern idiom*, spreads before us a panorama of Negro life to be found nowhere else in American literature. [Italics added]

It is this image of Tolson as the crusading modernist poet that has obscured the strength and intricacy of his roots in the Harlem Renaissance.

The relationship between universality and ethnicity in Tolson's work lends itself to much sophisticated now you see it, now you don't. Allen Tate in his introduction to Tolson's *Libretto for the Republic of Liberia* comments:

> It seems to me only common sense to assume that the main thing is the poetry, if one is a poet, whatever one's color may be. I think that Mr. Tolson assumed this; and the assumption, I gather, has made him no less but more intensely Negro in his apprehension of the world than any of his contemporaries, or any that I have read. But by becoming more intensely Negro he seems to me to dismiss the entire problem, so far as poetry is concerned, by putting it in its properly subordinate place. In the end I found that I was reading *Libretto for the Republic of Liberia* not because Mr. Tolson is a Negro but because he is a poet, not because the poem has a "Negro subject" but because it is about the world of all men. And this subject is not merely asserted; it is embodied in a rich and complex language, and realized in terms of the poetic imagination.[23]

Yet Dan McCall in his review of *The Libretto* sees Tolson's achievement in revolutionary terms. He applies Jean-Paul Sartre's observations on the African poet in "Black Orpheus" to Tolson:

> "It is when he seems suffocated by the serpents of our culture that he shows himself the most revolutionary, for he then undertakes to ruin systematically the European acquisition, and the demolition in spirit symbolizes the great, future taking up of arms by which the Negroes will break their chains." Tolson breaks his chains with bolts of laughter. There is in the *Libretto* an exuberant spirit proper to the occasion of mastering the white man's power and turning it back on him: see how I

23. Allen Tate, "Introduction," *Libretto for the Republic of Liberia* (New York: Twayne Publishers, Inc., 1953).

master the master. At times Tolson seems to be running wild in the white castle of learning. You have made me, he is saying, a black thief in the night; I am a Negro and have made my meals on what I hooked from your white kitchens and now that I have made my way into your study—see here—I walked off with your library . . . .

But to get simply the outrageous comic effect is not to get enough, for the outrage is in the service of a revolutionary possibility. Tolson is not just turning back on the white culture its own methods; he does it in the name of a new culture.[24]

Karl Shapiro uses Tolson's work as a principal argument in his quarrel with Tate and Eliot:

The falsification I speak of is that of trying to assimilate Tolson into the tradition when he was doing the opposite. The fact that Tolson's *Libretto* is unknown by white traditionalists gives the lie to the critic's assertion that Tolson has risen above Negro experience to become an "artist." The facts are that Tolson is a dedicated revolutionist who revolutionizes modern poetry in a language of American negritude. The forms of the *Libretto* and of *Harlem Gallery*, far from being "traditional," are the Negro satire upon the poetic tradition of the Eliots and Tates. The tradition cannot stand being satirized and lampooned and so tries to kick an authentic poet upstairs into the oblivion of acceptance. But the Negro artist won't stay in the attic anymore than he stayed in the cellar.[25]

Nathan Huggins, in his study of the Harlem Renaissance, gives only passing reference to Tolson, but his comment seems intended as high praise, although ironically its logic seems very close to that of Allen Tate's:

There is no quarrel that great literature is generated by ethos. Immigrants in the United States, as well as blacks, found their special condition a natural source of literature. Immigrants however, seemed to feel more free than blacks to write about themselves. Judging by Mary Astin, Abraham Cahan, and Michael Gold, Americanization was really the American story. Blacks, on the other hand, were plagued by a sense of being anomalous. The artistic question remained whether a work of art was a window opening onto an ethnic province—peculiar and curious—or whether through it the viewer could be drawn into a geography of his own humanity regardless of ethos. Recent writers—Bellow, Ellison, Malamud, Tolson— exemplify the possibilities. Through their works, the reader is taken through the "province" into the world at large. Also, art

24. Dan McCall, "The Quicksilver Sparrow of M. B. Tolson," *American Quarterly* 17:4 (Fall 1966): 541.
25. Karl Shapiro, "Decolonization of American Literature," *Wilson Library Bulletin* (June 1965): 853.

270

as craft defies parochialism. For there is pure pleasure in the discovery of a brilliant artistic conception, well constructed so that it holds together and works. Melvin Tolson's *Harlem Gallery* gives us such delight, independent of its ethnic center. The jazzmen of the 1920's seemed to understand all of this perfectly well. But for the contemporary black writer to do the same, he would have to lose the self-consciousness that made him a black man who wrote poems and novels (the same could be said for the Hoosier, the Yankee, the Jew, the Southerner, the woman, or what have you). One had to lose that self-consciousness, or rather, transform it into the very instrument that could slice through the boundaries that defined it.[26]

Melvin Tolson frequently asserted an "I-ness" that could not be encompassed by his "Negro-ness," but he never needed to think of himself as white, and he was proud of the ability of his people to survive and achieve. He knew that it took wit, courage, and sophistication, and he believed that the world was wide open for him to learn from, or if it was not wide open he was going to do his damnedest to make it so for him and those to follow. He wrote a speech that he planned to give on the one hundredth anniversary of the Emancipation Proclamation. Some of his phrases correspond suggestively to the titles of the four books he projected for his final *Harlem Gallery*:

> Between the Egypt Land of the antebellum South and the Promised Land of the Great Emancipator stretched a labyrinth in which the black man discovered no cloud by day and no pillar of fire by night. Yet, let us remember at this hour the apocalyptic words of Abe Lincoln: "If you don't know where you came from you don't know where you're going." That's the imperative reason why we must study Negro history, Negro art, Negro music. True, we have not yet reached the sublime heights of twenty-one major civilizations pictured by the great Toynbee in his ten giant volumes. Yet, we must remember what the heroic Frederick Douglass said to the slave masters: "Don't judge me by the height I have reached, but by the depth from which I come." Douglass said these words again and again, from pulpits, from auction blocks, from tombstones in graveyards.[27]

Tolson concluded this speech by quoting from Paul Laurence Dunbar's "Ode to Ethiopia":

> Go on and up! Our souls and eyes
> Shall follow thy continuous rise;
>   Our ears shall list thy story
> From bards who from thy roots shall spring,

26. Nathan I. Huggins, *Harlem Renaissance* (New York: Oxford University Press, 1971), pp. 200–201.
27. Tolson, "The Foreground of Negro Poetry," *Kansas Quarterly* (Summer 1975): 31.

And proudly tune their lyres to sing
  Of Ethiopia's glory.

Tolson's literary career suggests that this admonition constantly sounded in his own mind. He traveled on and up an extraordinary distance. Did he wander from the true path by listening to the Siren strains of Eliot and the New Critics, or did he break through to an advanced level of achievement and artistic sophistication with which the literary world has not yet caught up? It is too soon to answer that question with final authority and confidence. Those who have appreciated and understood how far he traveled have been too few, but they have often been persons of discernment and literary authority. We need to walk the roads Tolson actually did travel with greater attention to his signposts and his destination. It is to be hoped that the publication of this early book of poems about Harlem will help in establishing some of the markers and the principal directions of Melvin B. Tolson's literary journey. In addition to these important scholarly-critical goals, it is to be confidently expected that these poems will provide a rich and vibrant pleasure of their own.

Biographical and Bibliographical Notes

Melvin B. Tolson was born in Moberly, Missouri, on February 6, 1898. His father, Rev. Alonzo Tolson, was a Methodist minister who was assigned various churches in small towns of northern Missouri and southern Iowa until the family moved to Independence, Missouri, in approximately 1915. Alonzo was a strong speaker and an austere man who prided himself on having learned Latin and Greek, although he never attended college. Melvin frequently wrote affectionately of his "little walnut-hued mother," Lera Hurt Tolson. In a notebook he described his mother's family as "antebellum fugitives who hid themselves on the islands in the Mark Twain country and in the glooms of the Ozarks, from which they raided at midnight the slave plantations along the Missouri and Mississippi."

Tolson's first published poem appeared in the "Poet's Corner" of the town paper in Oskaloosa, Iowa, in 1912. At Lincoln High School in Kansas City, Missouri, he was chosen class poet, captain of the football team, and director and actor in the Greek Club's Little Theatre.

He attended Fisk University for one year, but in 1920 transferred to Lincoln University, Oxford, Pennsylvania, where he won awards in speech, debate, dramatics, and classical literature as well as again captaining the football team. A year and a half before he graduated with honors, he married Ruth Southall of Virginia on January 29, 1922. This marriage continued for the rest of his life.

In 1924 he began teaching at Wiley College, Marshall, Texas. He remained at Wiley until 1947. During this period the Tolsons had four children: Melvin Beaunorus, Jr., Arthur Lincoln, Wiley Wilson, and Ruth Marie.

Tolson was an extraordinarily successful teacher, debate coach, and director of drama. His debate teams lost only one debate in ten years, and he took them on extended tours, challenging the debate teams of black colleges and universities in the South and major integrated universities of the West. He organized an intercollegiate dramatic association and took his players into dramatic competitions in the North as well as in the South.

During the thirties he helped organize sharecroppers, both white and black, but insulated his family from these activities as much as possible for their own protection. In 1930–1931, his family lived with his parents at Kansas City while he took a year's leave from Wiley to work on a master's degree in comparative literature at Columbia University.

Throughout his early years at Wiley he wrote both poetry and prose, but he had little success getting his work into print until the late

273

thirties. V. F. Calverton published several individual poems from "A Gallery of Harlem Portraits" in *Modern Monthly* and *The Modern Quarterly*. On November 10, 1937, the Washington *Tribune* carried Tolson's first column titled "Caviar and Cabbage." This weekly column appeared regularly until May 15, 1943, and commented on a wide variety of topics concerning black life. In 1939 "Dark Symphony" won first place in a national poetry contest sponsored by the American Negro Exposition in Chicago. Two years later it was published in *Atlantic Monthly*.

Tolson's first book of collected poems, *Rendezvous with America*, was published in 1944, and in 1947 President V. S. Tubman appointed Tolson poet laureate of Liberia. That same year Tolson also decided to leave Wiley College and to accept a position as professor of English and drama at Langston University, Langston, Oklahoma. In 1953 Tolson published his *Libretto for the Republic of Liberia*.

In 1954, he received much recognition. He was awarded an honorary doctor of letters by his alma mater, Lincoln University, and later that year Ambassador Simpson of Liberia conferred upon him the Order of the Star of Africa. He was elected mayor of Langston, and he became a permanent Bread Loaf Fellow in poetry and drama, beginning a prized association with Robert Frost. He was reelected mayor three times before deciding not to run again.

In the later years of his life, Tolson projected a major epic poem concerned with the history and identity of the Negro in America. *Harlem Gallery, Book I: The Curator*, published in 1965, was the first of a projected five books. *Harlem Gallery* won Tolson major recognition. Unfortunately he was already engaged in a gallant, but eventually losing, struggle for his life with cancer. He had had two operations in 1964, but he refused to give up. He accepted the first appointment to the Avalon Chair in Humanities at Tuskegee Institute in 1965 and accepted a second honorary degree, the doctor of humane letters, from Lincoln University. He gave a reading at the Library of Congress under the auspices of the Gertrude Clarke Whittall Poetry and Literature Fund, and in May of 1966 he received the annual poetry award of the American Academy of Arts and Letters.

He died August 29, 1966, in St. Paul's Hospital, Dallas, Texas.

In an interview printed in *Anger and Beyond*, Tolson refers to *A Gallery of Harlem Portraits* as a manuscript of 340 pages. We now have a typescript with pages numbered only to 297, and some of these pages are missing. The available typescript shows evidence of partial revisions made by Tolson.

The opening poem, "Harlem," appears in the typescript on pages 10, 11, and 11½. Essentially the same poem, with its parts rearranged, appears as pages 1 and 2. These pages have been placed in the Appendix. The poems, "Joshua Granite" and "Marzimmu Heffner" appear twice in the typescript. I have chosen what seems to be the later versions for the main text and included the earlier versions in the Appendix. In the typescript there is an extra poem, "Cato Snoddy," appearing on pages numbered 112 and 113, although the final page of "Zip Lightner" and the entire poem "Old Pettigrew" also appear on pages with those numbers. I have included "Cato Snoddy" in the Appendix. Misspellings and obvious typographical errors have been corrected from the original typescript.

Several individual poems from *A Gallery of Harlem Portraits* have been published in magazines. "Jacob Nollen," *Modern Monthly* (May 1937), p. 10, and "Dr. Harvey Whyte," *Modern Monthly* (August 1937), p. 10, were published as they appear in this text. Only the last portion of "Uncle Walt" appeared under that title in *The Modern Quarterly* (March 1938), p. 10. "The Underdog" was published as "Kikes, Bohunks, Crackers, Dagos, Niggers," in *The Modern Quarterly* (Autumn 1939), pp. 18–19. A shortened variation of the first part of "Harlem," the opening poem of this manuscript, appeared as "Vergil Ragsdale" in *The Modern Quarterly* (Winter 1939), p. 48. This is not to be confused with the poem titled "Vergil Ragsdale" in the present text. I have added "Hamuel Gutterman," *The Modern Quarterly* (April 1937), p. 7, to this book, although it is not in the typescript of *A Gallery* that is on file at the Library of Congress. References to Gutterman and to his position in the Harlem Hotel in "Ferenc Glaspell" suggest that "Hamuel Gutterman" probably is on the missing page 119 of the typescript.

Other poems have appeared in *New Letters* and *Y'Bird* in more recent years. "Sootie Joe," "Peg Leg Snelson," "Jobyna Dear," "Black Moses," and "Freemon Hawthorne" were published in *New Letters* (Summer 1976), pp. 164–69. "Chittling Sue," "Pearl Tripplett," "Lena Lovelace," "Augustus Lence," "Flora Murdock," and "The Underdog," were published in *New Letters* (Spring 1977), pp. 11–18.

The following poems were published in 1978 in *Y'Bird* I, 2, pp. 82–97: "Grandma Lonigan," "Margaret Levy," "Daddy Oldfield," "Sarah Ashton," "Steve Wordsworth," "Lady Hope," "Black Zuleika," "Babe Quest," "Grand Chancellor Knapp Sackville," "Editor Crum," "Miss Felicia Babcock," "Abraham Dumas," "Senola Hurse," "Jack Patterson," and "Stillicho Spikes."

The typescript for *A Gallery of Harlem Portraits* is in the Melvin B. Tolson Collection in the Library of Congress.

David Ray, friend and colleague, introduced me to Ruth S. Tolson, and I first saw many of Tolson's unpublished manuscripts at her home in Washington, D. C., in the spring of 1973. Ruth Marie, Tolson's daughter, a professional librarian and a warm and gracious human being, had organized the manuscripts and helped me to copy much of the material to consider for eventual publication.

On March 18, 1976, Ruth Marie, like her father, died of cancer. It is because of her care for her father's work and because of her generous help to me that this book is dedicated to her memory.

I would also like to acknowledge with gratitude the financial help of the University of Missouri–Kansas City Graduate School Research Council for enabling me to visit the Tolson home in 1973, and to thank Alma Hill and Teresa Young of U.M.K.C. who typed much of this manuscript.